GF406272

UNBREAKABLE

FROM BLACK SHEEP TO O1E

DIANA M. MARTIN

For every black sheep who walked through fire and still
found the courage to rise.

For the little girl I once was and the woman I fought to become.

For my daughter, the heartbeat of my legacy, the reason I kept going
even when I didn't recognize myself.

And for anyone who has ever felt unseen, unheard, or unprotected,
may these pages remind you that your story is not over.

You are still becoming!

You are unbreakable!

Table of Contents

Acknowledgements

This book was written from a place of truth, not perfection.

It is not a how-to guide, a tell-all, or a polished retelling meant to provide comfort. It is a lived account of survival, healing, motherhood, leadership, and becoming - written in real time, with honesty and care. Some names, details, and identifying elements have been changed to protect privacy, but the emotional truth remains intact.

This story is mine, but it was not lived alone.

I acknowledge the women who held space for me when I couldn't hold myself. The mentors who saw my leadership before I did. The Sailors who trusted me, challenged me, and reminded me why presence matters more than rank. The friends who celebrated my becoming and stayed when it wasn't convenient. And the therapists, counselors, and quiet professionals who helped me learn how to feel without drowning.

Most of all, this book is for my daughter.

Every word written here carries her future in mind. May she grow knowing she does not have to earn love through sacrifice, silence, or survival. May she know that healing is allowed, joy is not a betrayal, and choosing yourself is an act of courage.

If you are reading this and recognize pieces of yourself here, know this: you are not alone, and you are not broken. This book is not meant to fix you - it is meant to remind you of what is already within you.

Thank you for witnessing this story.

CHAPTER 1

THE SILENCE IN THE WALLS

The air that morning carried more than silence-it carried memory. I couldn't quite name the thickness in it; part silence, part memory, part warning. Somewhere in the distance, a dog barked, its echo bouncing lazily through the neighborhood, before fading as if it had sunk into the damp earth itself. The faint scent of rain clung to the ground, mixing with the earthy smell of grass, the metallic tang of wet pavement, and the old wood of apartment doors. Even the air seemed tired, like it had been holding secrets for too long.

My shoulders tightened, a dull ache settling in, the kind that crept up when I was trying too hard to look unaffected. I remember digging my fingernails into my palms to keep myself moving, each step forward deliberate, not just in distance but in determination, a silent promise to myself that this moment would mean something, even if I had to drag meaning out of the thin air. I remember the chipped paint on the doorframe, flakes catching the light like old confetti, the squeak of the hinges when they opened, the uneven rhythm of my own breathing. Those tiny details became anchors, proof that I was still present, even when I wanted to disappear.

Growing up, the walls of our house seemed to carry every sound: my sister's laughter, my mother's tired footsteps, the hum of the television that stayed on too late at night. The kitchen smelled like whatever we could make stretch for the week, sometimes fried chicken, sometimes noodles and butter. I can still picture the couch with its worn cushions and the way sunlight hits the living room in the mornings, making everything look softer than it really was. Those details formed the backdrop of my childhood, and even now, certain smells or songs can take me right back there.

If my grandmother was my first bully, then my mother was the one who made me question why I was never enough.

As a little girl, I didn't know what stability looked like, but I knew what it felt like to live without it. I would visit friends' houses and notice the way their parents talked to each other, the meals laid out on their tables, the calm that seemed to live in their walls. Then I would come home and feel the difference like a weight pressing on my chest. It wasn't that I didn't have love. I did, but it came with storms too, and I learned early how to weather them.

She didn't raise me, not really. We were taken away from her when I was about four or five. That memory sits quietly until something stirs it; a scent or a sound and suddenly I'm back there again. It felt like we had become an obligation she couldn't manage anymore. Instead of raising her children, she raised her boyfriend's two. We saw her on the weekends, when she made time. At work, she seemed untouchable; at home, she vanished.

We lived in a cramped two-bedroom apartment. My mom worked long nights and was rarely around, so my older sister watched us. But protection was never part of that arrangement. She brought people into our home, people who didn't belong there. Loud voices. Sharp cologne. Music too loud. Smoke that never cleared. I learned early that my comfort ranked last.

The walls pressed in, the ceilings low enough to feel heavy. The smell of old takeout mixed with cigarette smoke lingered no matter how much the windows were cracked. Even then, I was learning to breathe through the smoke and call it air. I remember sitting in corners while strangers filled the living room, wishing myself invisible. Sometimes I wanted to ask her to make them leave, to give me back even a sliver of safety, but I already knew my voice didn't matter…

Strangers were constantly in our space.

Grown men.

Loud music.

Smoke.

Chaos.

I never felt safe, not even in my own home. It felt like growing up in the cracks, trying to stay out of the way, trying not to be noticed so I wouldn't get hurt. Sometimes they would hit or beat us with socks, and laugh like it was nothing. I hated when my sister was in charge. Her needs always came first, even when it cost us our innocence.

We were all surviving in our own ways. My older sister carried too much responsibility too soon, and I stopped feeling safe around her. I built emotional walls early.

There were moments I felt completely invisible. I learned to read a room before anyone spoke. I knew when to hide. When to be still. That was survival.

At night, I rehearsed words I never said out loud. *Protect me. See me. Choose me.* But my voice stayed trapped in my throat.

I became the helper.

The peacekeeper.

The one who swallowed emotions so no one else had to carry them.

No one came to save me.

I had to be everything I needed.

The apartment itself seemed to learn our fear. Every creak, every shadow carried memory. The faded carpet smelled faintly musty, worn down by years of use. The refrigerator hummed constantly, its sides warm to the touch. Light filtered through yellowed blinds that swayed whenever a neighbor's door slammed. Even the light felt tired.

I found strange comfort in the office where my mother worked. Fluorescent lights. The scent of paper and toner. The quiet tapping of keyboards. It felt far removed from home. I would sit in a corner, legs tucked under me, imagining that if I stayed quiet enough, I could blend into that calm forever. Those early mornings made me feel older than I was, learning silence, learning how adults survive behind artificial light.

At the time, I didn't realize I was building armor: every ignored question, every broken promise stitched together another layer. I learned how to smile without showing the hurt, a skill that followed me into adulthood.

Silence wasn't peace in that apartment. It was the sound of being overlooked. There were no bedtime stories, no emotional check-ins—just survival. Silence meant listening for footsteps, for a door unlocking, for breathing you didn't recognize. I learned to control my own breath, to press my ear against the wall just close enough to hear without being seen. Quiet taught me how to perform calmly, even when fear lived in my chest.

My mother would drift in and out like a distant relative. And still, I craved her. I wanted her to choose me. To see me as more than a chore. I remember watching her in her office, high up in that building, composed, respected, smelling like paper and perfume. For a moment, I admired her. That version of her didn't exist at home.

Sometimes she smelled like liquor and smoke, and that version made me shrink. I once whispered, 'Mama, can we just stay home tonight?" She looked at me like I had asked for the moon. That moment confirmed what I already knew. I wasn't her priority.

She could sit feet away from me and still feel miles distant. I knew her schedule, her footsteps, her perfume, but I didn't know her. Not really. I wanted a version of her that didn't exist. A mother who noticed when I went quiet. Who offered comfort without me breaking first. Instead, I got fragments.

There were always men. Always moments where she vanished into someone else's world, leaving me to navigate mine alone. Even as a child, I understood that I was the background. The afterthought. The one who had to hold herself together.

That lesson stayed with me. It taught me to perform. To be useful. To not need too much. It taught me that love could exist and still be unavailable.

Despite everything, there were moments when life felt simple. Halloween was one of them.

Costumes. Laughter. The chance to be someone else for a night. We walked the neighborhood shouting, "Trick or treat," pillowcases growing heavy with candy. For once, I felt like every other kid.

When we got home, my mom carefully sorted the candy, dividing it into little bags to make it last. In those moments, the house felt lighter. The walls loosened their grip. Halloween reminded me that joy could still sneak in, even when life was messy.

I kept telling myself I was fine, but my mouth tasted like pennies, and my shoulders were tight with habit. Strength, back then, meant swallowing words whole and smiling with a full stomach. I didn't yet know that courage could sound like a quiet no or a door closing behind me.

I hated when my mom went to work; we were left to fend for ourselves. I didn't understand it then. I was just a kid, but I wished she could have been home more. We did find moments of fun. We had a dog. I can't remember his name, and we'd have him chase us around the house to pass the time on nights she wasn't there.

I didn't spend much time with my mom as a child. She kept me home often and said I cried all the time. When it was finally time for me to go to school, I struggled to adjust. She had to sit in class with me until one day I was okay without her. That was around the time we moved in with my grandmother.

I learned early how to listen for what wasn't being said, the pain behind laughter, the exhaustion behind smiles.

Looking back now, I see how I measured safety by how small I could make myself. It took years to learn that shrinking isn't peace. It's a slow erasure. The day I stopped apologizing for taking up space was the day the room finally felt like mine.

Those early years gave me a crash course in resilience. I didn't understand it then, but I was already learning how to adjust, how to keep going, how to read people's energy before they spoke. That survival skill would follow me into the Navy, into motherhood, and into every relationship I had.

I didn't just grow up in that house.

I trained there.

CHAPTER 2

APPEARANCES

We went to a nice school once we moved in with my grandmother and grandfather. It was called Jessie P. Miller. I was in kindergarten, still small enough to believe adults always meant well, still learning how to sit still, raise my hand, and trust that someone would come back for me at the end of the day. The school was predominantly white, and at the time, race wasn't something I had language for yet. I didn't know how to name the difference, only that my life didn't look like everyone else's.

My grandparents' house felt permanent in a way nothing before it had. My grandmother ran everything. My grandfather was there, too quiet, present, and absent at the same time. He saw what happened in that house. He said nothing. I didn't understand then that silence could be a choice.

At school, I noticed differences in small ways, the calm in other kids' voices when they talked about home. The way their parents showed up without warning. The softness that seemed to live in their walls. I learned early how to adjust, how to blend in, how to perform.

From the outside, our lives looked good. We had pressed clothes. Someone did our laundry. Someone ironed our uniforms. We had a driver who took us to the Boys and Girls Club, to hair appointments, wherever we needed to go. We went on field trips. We showed up to school events. People assumed we were lucky. Spoiled, even.

And in some ways, we were.

But privilege only lived in appearances. Outsiders saw pressed clothes; we felt the weight of walking on eggshells. They saw routine and assumed safety. They didn't smell the bleach that clung to our hands after scrubbing floors or hear the sting of words that cut deeper than any chore. They didn't step into the kitchen at midnight when the air was heavy with silence and fear.

I remember lying awake some nights, my small body stiff under the covers, listening for footsteps. Every creak of the floorboards sounded like a warning. Sometimes I pressed my pillow over my ears to muffle the sound of shouting. Other times, I stared into the dark, counting seconds until the house went still again. That kind of fear didn't fade with the sunrise. It stayed tucked in my chest, teaching me to read a room before I even stepped into it.

School became my refuge.

I blended in well with my peers, but sometimes I would sit in the corner and rock back and forth. Sometimes I would cry. Sometimes my classmates would console me. I remember my teacher used to sing to me:

"You are my sunshine, my only sunshine. You make me happy when the skies are gray…"

Her voice was gentle, a lullaby in a place where comfort was scarce. I would close my eyes and let the song wrap around me like a blanket. In those moments, I felt chosen, seen in a way home never allowed. It showed me tenderness could exist, even in small doses.

I loved school. I looked forward to it. Books were my escape, my comfort, and my voice when I didn't feel like I had one. I disappeared into stories and, for a while, forgot that my life was unstable.

I did everything I could to excel. In first grade, I wrote a book called *My Candy Car*. I wanted a car made entirely of candy. By third grade, we had to change schools because my twin brother and sister were always getting in trouble. I was heartbroken. The new school was more diverse, and I was nervous, but once I met my classmates, those feelings eased.

I still felt like I had to be perfect.

My first "play" boyfriend was a boy named Max. He was cute. We played together every day and napped side by side during rest time. We shared crayons, giggled when our hands brushed. It was innocent and small, but to me, it mattered. It was the first time I learned that connection could be soft.

I remember running up to my grandmother with my report card, straight A's, honor roll, and my blue certificate in hand. I was smiling.

"What's your little black ugly ass smiling at?" she said.

"You still going to be nothing?"

My smile dropped. I ran to the room I shared with my siblings and cried. I begged God to take me away. I don't remember a time when I felt like I was enough.

Trying to be perfect only made things worse.

Even when I was awarded Youth of the Year at the Boys and Girls Club, back-to-back, it still wasn't enough. Nothing ever was. Everyone saw it. Everyone heard it. No one did anything. Not even my mother, who we only saw on weekends, said a word.

People looked at us and envied our lives. They saw clean clothes. New shoes. A nice house. A structured routine.

They didn't see the cost.

CHAPTER 3

NO MARKS

As a kid, no matter how hard I tried, how well I did, or how much I poured myself into proving I was worth something, the response was always the same: belittled, ridiculed, dismissed. People often say, "Our grandparents raised us differently." And that's true. But different doesn't always mean right.

My grandmother was strict. Not "sit up straight and mind your manners" strict. She was the kind of strict that made you feel small just for breathing too loudly. I feared her. Absolutely. And not the kind of fear rooted in respect. This was the kind that made your stomach knot when her footsteps hit the hallway.

She'd hit me with anything.

A belt.

A switch.

A shoe.

Whatever was closest.

Most of the time, I hadn't even done anything. I just *was*. And for her, that was too much. Existing in a body she didn't understand, with emotions she didn't care to hold, was enough to be punished for.

She had belts with her name carved into them, like weapons stamped with ownership. Punishment didn't require guilt. If one of us messed up, all of us paid. I learned early that fairness didn't live in our home.

Eventually, I stopped crying.

Eventually, the hits stopped stinging.

My body learned to absorb pain the same way my spirit did-quietly. When she noticed that, she changed her tactics. She reached for whatever else could hurt.

I remember riding with her to the bus stop one morning in middle school. I could've walked, but she insisted on driving and then resented having to do it. She cursed me out before I even sat down. I hadn't said a word. I hadn't done anything. She just let the venom spill, word after word, as if it were my fault she was angry, tired, and disappointed with life.

Then I heard a boom.

And then we crashed.

Just like that.

I lay there in the front seat, frozen. And in that moment, I decided to close my eyes and pretend to be unconscious. Not because I was hurt, but because I needed a break. From her. From everything.

The silence of the ambulance was the safest I had felt in a long time.

Church was her stage.

Every Sunday, she transformed into someone else, a woman who spoke softly, smiled sweetly, and walked with the grace of a godly matriarch. I used to watch her hands, steady and elegant as she passed out peppermints, her smile wide and convincing. And I would wonder how those same hands that held peppermints so gently could also hold belts that left welts.

That contradiction lived in my body. It taught me early that two things could be true at once and that appearances could be a lie.

The same woman who screamed at me for breathing too loudly would suddenly be praising the Lord with a gentle hum, handing out candy as if she were made of sugar. And us? We were her props.

Perfect little porcelain dolls.

Matching frilly dresses.

Lace socks.

Baby doll shoes.

Hair pressed.

Bows tight.

She even gave us little purses, even if they were empty. Because this wasn't about us, it was about her image. We weren't being raised. We were being presented.

I remember sitting stiffly in the pews, not allowed to slouch or speak unless spoken to. We had to smile. Always. Not because we were happy, but because we were supposed to be.

Looking "put together" mattered more than being okay.

People at church adored her.

"Your grandmother is a blessing."

"She's doing such a good job with you girls."

I would nod. But inside, I'd think, if *only you knew*.

Because the moment we pulled out of the church parking lot, literally the second, the softness disappeared. Her tone snapped back like a rubber band. I knew I'd be punished for something. Maybe the way I sat. Maybe a whisper to my sister. Maybe nothing at all.

But it was coming.

She had two faces. One for them. One for us.

That kind of duality does something to a child. It makes you question your reality. It makes you doubt your feelings. If everyone else sees her as kind and nurturing, then maybe *I'm* the problem. Maybe I'm too much. Too emotional. Too sensitive.

It took years for me to realize I wasn't broken. I was surviving someone else's performance.

Growing up with her taught me to split myself, too. There was the version of me that performed polished, respectful, never questioning. And then there was the real me: quiet, scared, always walking on emotional eggshells.

I became a master at reading moods. Adjusting my tone and shrinking my needs. It was the only way to survive in a house where love had conditions and anger had no warning.

I stopped trying to be heard.

I stopped crying when it hurt.

I stopped expecting comfort because comfort never came.

I carried that survival into everything.

Friendships. Relationships. Motherhood. The mirror. I became everything I thought I needed to be to avoid rejection, to avoid punishment, to keep people pleased even if it cost me myself.

The church confused me deeply. People lifted their hands in worship while I sat beside her, wondering how someone could be so cruel behind closed doors and still be seen as holy. If this was what God looked like, I didn't want Him. If being "good" meant smiling through pain and hiding the truth, I wanted no part of it.

I didn't want faith that made room for her performance but not for my pain.

So I disconnected. I sat through sermons without listening. I bowed my head without praying. I endured, just as I did at home.

But God found me anyway.

Not in a pew.

Not through her voice.

But in silence.

After the storm.

In the stillness of my brokenness, I felt something real. Not punishment. Not performance. Just grace. Quiet, soft grace. I realized I didn't have to be perfect to be loved. I didn't have to carry guilt to have faith. I didn't have to fear God the way I feared her.

That's the faith I hold onto now. Not religion.

Relationship.

It wasn't all pain.

Every year, my grandmother would pull us out of school for the state fair. For one day, we were free. Funnel cakes. Rides. Laughter. The wind in my hair. The world felt bigger, lighter. I clung to those moments like life rafts, proof that joy was possible.

But structure always followed.

Our lives looked good from the outside. Driver. Clean clothes. Ironed uniforms. But we also scrubbed carpets on our knees with red-bristled brushes and bottles of Resolve. My grandmother had a ritual. The carpet had to shine no matter how tired we were.

That was life with her. Hard. Controlled. Not gentle, but consistent.

She worked. My grandfather worked. Yet they were strangers under one roof. They didn't sleep together. I never saw affection. He saw everything. He said nothing.

Some wounds don't get closure. Some people never apologize. But I know now I didn't deserve any of it.

When the pain stopped showing, she noticed. So I learned to fake cry. I learned that what mattered was that there were no marks.

Everything else was fair game.

I'm grateful she took us in. I'm grateful for the roof, the food, and the structure. She did what she knew how to do. But her methods were trauma dressed up as discipline.

And still, I survived

CHAPTER 4

HIDING IN BOOKS

The air that morning was cool but restless, brushing against my skin with the faint smell of rain before it even fell. Light filtered through the blinds in fractured stripes, marking the walls like gentle reminders of the day waiting outside. Every sound felt amplified in that stillness, the hum of the refrigerator, the faint ticking of the clock in the kitchen, and the steady pull of my own breath.

I was that girl.

The one who tore through books like they were lifelines.

In many ways, they were.

I read the entire library by the time I left elementary school. Shelf after shelf, spine after spine, every story gave me air. The library became my sanctuary. Walking through the aisles felt like stepping into a protected world where no one could touch me. The shelves towered above me like guardians, lined with spines that whispered promises of escape. I traced my fingers along the worn covers, inhaling the mix of paper, ink, and dust, and for a moment, it felt like breathing in freedom.

At home, I felt small.

Inside those walls, surrounded by endless stories, I felt infinite.

It wasn't just a hobby. It was home.

I was an accelerated reader, top of my class in points, and I lived for those pizza parties, the reward for reading more than anyone else. Those pizza parties might have seemed insignificant to everyone else, but to me, they were everything. Sitting at a table in the library with a greasy slice on a paper plate felt like recognition. For once, I wasn't invisible or overlooked. I was celebrated.

I remember the way the cheese stretched as I pulled the first bite, the chatter of classmates fading as I basked in the quiet pride of being seen. That pizza wasn't just food, it was validation. In that library, I found what home never gave me: permission to feel noticed.

While other kids played outside, I was tucked into corners with *The Babysitters Club*, *Goosebumps*, and any mystery I could handle. I wanted to be Claudia. I wanted to solve spooky crimes in creepy towns. And when I discovered Mary Higgins Clark and James Patterson, something clicked. My heart found its rhythm in their pages.

I daydreamed about becoming a detective, sneaking through neighborhoods with a notepad in hand, convinced I could solve mysteries no one else could untangle. Other times, I imagined myself as the writer, spinning stories powerful enough to pull someone else out of their reality, the way books had saved me. Those daydreams gave me hope that there was more waiting for me beyond the four walls I lived in.

I can still remember the smell of old library books—ink, dust, and something almost magical that clung to the pages. Sometimes my fingers came away gray from worn covers, but I didn't care. Each book was a portal. When I opened a *Babysitters Club* book, I could imagine myself in Claudia's room, surrounded by art supplies and friends planning adventures, instead of sitting quietly trying to tune out my real life.

Goosebumps gave me permission to be afraid in a way that had an ending, unlike the fear that lived in my body daily.

I didn't always understand every grown-up word, but I understood the feelings: suspense, fear, hope, grit. I lived those emotions in real life without resolution. Reading gave me what life didn't: control, answers, endings that made sense. It was the one thing no one could take from me. Not my mother's absence. Not my grandmother's discipline. Not the chaos in the house.

Books were mine.

In a world where I often felt too sensitive, too invisible, too much in those pages, I was just right. I underlined words I didn't know, mouthed them quietly, and guessed their meaning before running to a dictionary. Every new word felt like power. The suspense taught me to expect twists, to stay alert, to read between the lines-skills I didn't yet know I was practicing for life.

In school, I was praised for my achievements. For understanding concepts. For delivering perfect work. I became addicted to validation through success, as if excellence were the only way to earn my place in the world. And still, no matter how much I achieved, something felt just out of reach, a sense of belonging not tied to grades or performance.

Books became more than an escape.

They became survival.

I curled into corners with stories and imagined myself anywhere but there. I hid under blankets with flashlights, heart racing not from the plot but from the possibility of being caught awake past bedtime. Those nights felt like stolen freedom. The hum of appliances and creak of floorboards became part of the soundtrack to my imaginary worlds.

As I grew, books gave me language for feelings I didn't know how to name. They gave me hope. They reminded me there was more beyond what I was living through and that maybe I was more than what I'd been told I was.

But books also helped me build walls.

I became so used to retreating inward that letting people see me felt dangerous. Vulnerability was foreign. Trust felt unsafe. I had learned early that love could be conditional and sharp, so I kept people at arm's length, even the ones who meant well.

On the outside, I looked strong. Focused. Put together.

On the inside, I was guarded, always bracing for the next critique, the next moment I'd be told I wasn't enough.

Perfectionism followed me everywhere. School. Work. Relationships. I held myself to impossible standards because being needed felt safer than being known. I took care of everyone else. I smiled through the pain. I rarely asked for help.

I was tired.

Tired of proving myself.

Tired of pretending I didn't hurt.

When I read about heartbreak, betrayal, and courage, I realized I wasn't alone in those feelings. Even fictional pain validated mine. Books whispered that pain didn't make me broken-it made me human.

Looking back now, it makes sense. Those hours buried in stories weren't just escape-they were training. I was learning how people think. How power shifts. How truth reveals itself slowly. I didn't know it then, but those authors shaped me. They taught me to observe, to listen between lines, to speak when it mattered.

Books taught me that silence can be loud.

That strength doesn't always scream.

That endurance is not weakness.

Those plot twists prepared me for the ones I'd live later, being betrayed, overlooked, underestimated, and still standing. Life became my longest novel, with chapters I never saw coming and no way to skip ahead. I had to live every word.

Books didn't just give me stories.

They gave me proof that survival could coexist with imagination.

But eventually, life would ask me to stop reading about bravery and start living it.

Books gave me somewhere to go when nowhere else felt safe. But they also taught me how to disappear so well that, over time, I forgot how to let people find me.

I learned how to retreat inward.

How to build a world no one else could touch.

It kept me alive.

It kept me quiet.

And for a long time, that felt like the same thing.

CHAPTER 5

FIRST LOVE, FIRST BREAK

The morning carried a crispness that hinted at change, the kind that rustles leaves before they fall. I didn't know it then, but I was standing at the edge of something that would shape me for years to come.

By the time I reached my teenage years, emotional suppression had already become second nature. I knew how to keep my face still, how to swallow feelings before they surfaced, how to move through the world without letting anyone see what I carried. Strength, to me, meant silence.

High school hallways were loud in a way that felt isolating. Lockers slammed. Sneakers squeaked against polished floors. Laughter bounced off the walls as it belonged to someone else's life. I walked with my books pressed tightly against my chest, gripping them like armor. The smell of metal and pencil shavings lingered in the air as couples passed by, fingers intertwined, heads leaned together in private jokes. I watched them with quiet longing. That was the world I wanted to belong to - a world where connection didn't have to be earned, where affection wasn't conditional.

Sometimes I imagined someone waiting for me at my locker, slipping their fingers through mine like it was the most natural thing in the world. I imagined laughter without perfection. But I kept walking. Belonging felt like a luxury I couldn't afford.

I didn't cry much. Not because I didn't hurt, but because I had trained myself to believe tears were weakness. I became the girl who smiled while breaking, who pushed through no matter how heavy things felt. I wore emotional armor so well that even I started believing it was real. Inside, though, I was exhausted.

That exhaustion showed up quietly. Lying awake at night, replaying conversations. Forcing myself out of bed each morning, layering on small talk and smiles like clothes I didn't want to wear. Laughing at jokes I didn't find funny. Agreeing just to keep the peace. By the end of the day, my face hurt from pretending. I wasn't just tired in my body - I was tired in my soul.

Trust was another casualty. I didn't trust people to protect me. I didn't trust love because I had learned it often came with conditions. When people showed me kindness, I waited for the switch - the moment warmth would turn cold. Compliments felt suspicious, like a setup for disappointment. Vulnerability felt dangerous. If I let someone see the cracks, everything might collapse.

So I became performance-based. If I could get good grades, be the good kid, check every box, maybe that would finally make me worthy of love. That belief followed me into friendships and eventually relationships.

I either kept people at a distance or attached too tightly. I wanted connection but feared abandonment. I became a chameleon - whoever I needed to be to feel accepted. Somewhere along the way, I lost track of who I actually was.

At dinner, forks clicked against plates while the television murmured from the other room. No one asked how I was. I cut my food into pieces too small to taste, managing the room so I didn't have to admit how invisible I felt. I remember wishing - just once - that someone would look across the table and say, *You don't have to carry it all.*

I showed up. I achieved. But no one saw the weight I carried.

By my mid-teens, the pressure felt suffocating. I don't remember the exact day, but I remember the feeling like the walls were closing in, every breath shallow. I didn't want to die. I just didn't want to hurt anymore. That was the first time I realized how deeply it had all scarred me.

I didn't have language for my pain, so I searched for belonging in the wrong places.

That's when my first relationship began.

I was still in High School, young, emotionally unprotected, desperate to feel chosen. He leaned against lockers with an easy grin, spoke softly late at night, and made promises that felt like oxygen. For the first time, someone paid attention to me. And I confused attention with love.

When you've never known safe love, even danger can look like devotion.

At first, it felt intoxicating, constant calls, endless messages, the feeling of being wanted. But slowly, the tone shifted. Questions turned into accusations. Curiosity became control. He checked my phone. Questioned my clothes.

"I just don't want other guys looking at you," he'd say, pulling me close.

I told myself it was love.

But it wasn't. It was possession dressed as care.

The relationship became emotionally abusive, not always with hands, but with words sharp enough to leave lasting marks. He tore me down and then acted like I was the reason. "I love you," followed by pain. That kind of manipulation rewires you. It makes you doubt your worth, your reality, your strength.

I learned to negotiate for peace. To rehearse apologies in the mirror. To soften my truth so it wouldn't cost me connection. Perfection became camouflage. If I asked for less, maybe he'd stay.

But I was disappearing.

One night, after another fight, I stood in front of the mirror and didn't recognize the girl staring back. Her shoulders were hunched. Her eyes were tired. The dreamer who used to escape into books was fading.

That was the moment I knew I had to leave.

Leaving wasn't dramatic. It was a quiet breaking point. Staying was destroying me faster than walking away ever could.

When I left, I didn't just leave him. I left the version of myself who thought love meant pain.

I left town. I left the weight. I left everything that had been suffocating me. I didn't have all the answers, but I knew I needed distance. I needed structure. Purpose. Something bigger than survival.

That's when I joined the Navy.

The Navy became both my escape and my foundation. For the first time, there was order. Expectations. Challenges that pushed my body and mind that didn't require me to disappear to survive. It wasn't easy, but it was different. Tangible. Honest.

Distance gave me space to breathe. To feel my strength returning. To believe that freedom wasn't selfish. It was necessary.

First love was supposed to be sweet—a pressed flower between pages. For me, it was the beginning of learning that love without boundaries can destroy you.

But even that heartbreak gave me something.

It showed me what self-abandonment looked like and taught me never to repeat it.

I didn't know it then, but I wasn't running away.

I was running toward myself.

CHAPTER 6

BAPTISM BY FIRE

Joining the Navy was the first real decision I made entirely on my own. It wasn't about running anymore; it was about rising. Boot camp was a shock to every part of my system. The early mornings, the sound of boots hitting the ground in unison, the metallic tang of sweat and disinfectant in the air, it was a world of discipline and survival.

The very first morning is seared into my memory. The shrill blast of the whistle shattered the silence, and in seconds the barracks erupted into chaos, boots slamming the floor, lockers clanging open, voices barking orders that felt too fast to follow. My hands shook as I tried to lace up my shoes, the pressure of a hundred recruits all stumbling, rushing, trying not to be the one who stood out for the wrong reason. I remember glancing at the faces around me, some hardened, some terrified, and realizing we were all strangers bound by the same fear of failing.

I learned quickly that hesitation was weakness. Every task, from folding a shirt to standing at attention, felt like a test of worth. I remember the first time I had to run, lungs burning, every muscle screaming, but deep down I felt fire building, a belief that I could endure anything. That run was more than a physical test; it was a battle with me. Every step pounded like an argument in my head: *quit, keep going, quit, keep going.* And with every choice to keep going, I felt like I was outrunning more than just a

25

timed course. I was outrunning every insult, every doubt, every voice that told me I wasn't enough.

The finish line wasn't just the end of a run, it was proof that my body and spirit could carry me further than my fear ever wanted me to go.

While I was rising professionally, I was unraveling internally. The ghosts of my past hadn't left; they'd just found quieter ways to haunt me.

My first deployment took me out to sea, and there's nothing quite like the vastness of the ocean surrounding you. The ship itself was a floating city, the constant hum of the engine, the cramped coffin stacked three high, the mess decks chatter. It was suffocating at times, yet strangely comforting, knowing everyone on board was living the same grind.

I felt a sense of unity, a strange kind of family, though I often kept my guard up. Some nights, I'd slip away to the weather decks to breathe. The wind whipped hard, salt stinging my face, and above me the sky stretched out like an endless black canvas scattered with stars. Out there, with nothing but water and sky in every direction, I felt both impossibly small and strangely limitless. That contradiction mirrored my own life, confined by circumstances, yet somehow destined for more. The ocean had a way of silencing everything, even the noise inside me. In those moments, I didn't feel like a Sailor or a scared girl trying to prove herself; I just felt human, suspended between the sea and the stars.

I would write letters to myself in my head, small promises that I wouldn't let this ship swallow who I was becoming.

Even in uniform, I was still that girl trying to prove she was enough, pouring myself into every task, every detail. I threw myself into the work, wanting to be the best and be seen for something other than my pain. I followed rules, rose through the ranks, and earned respect. But behind that strength was a woman still learning how to love herself. Still carrying old wounds, even as she built a new life.

The Navy gave me structure. It taught me responsibility, leadership, and how to operate under pressure. But it also distracted me from the more profound healing I hadn't yet done. I was surviving—and even thriving on the surface—but I hadn't slowed down long enough to address what still lived beneath.

The Navy gave me a fresh start—but even new beginnings don't erase old wounds. The pride of wearing the uniform, saluting the flag for colors, and hearing my name during promotions was real, but so was the weight of what I carried. Even as I built my reputation of resilience and strength, inside I was still haunted by memories I had no language for. The Navy gave me direction, but the shadows of my past followed me from boot camp to deployment, reminding me that achievements don't erase pain.

I was finally doing something for me, proving people wrong, checking off goals. I looked strong, and in many ways, I was. But I was still healing through movement. Still afraid of being alone and still craving a safe place to land. I joined the Navy in 2008. The uniform didn't just symbolize service; it represented a chance to rewrite everything I thought I knew about myself. I was young, determined, and terrified all at once.

Basic training came and went like a whirlwind. When I stepped into my first command—VAW 116 out of Point Mugu, California—I was just a Yeoman Seaman Recruit, the lowest enlisted rank. I didn't know what to expect. I only knew I had to succeed. I buried my fear beneath discipline and gave my all to the work. Whatever they needed done, I made it my mission to learn and deliver. Those early days were about proving myself—fast. Fear was real, but so was the drive to prove myself. Every doubt that whispered in my head was drowned out by the thought of becoming more than what life had handed me.

I didn't have time to ease into it. I deployed back-to-back in 2010 and 2011 aboard the USS Abraham Lincoln. Life on the ship was intense—long days, heavy workloads, constant motion. But I found a rhythm. I earned both my Surface and Air Warfare pins. I was named Blue Jacket of the Year. By the time I left that command, I had advanced to E5.

On paper, I was rising, I was thriving. But there was a different story behind the uniform and the accolades.

No one prepares you for the kind of pain that doesn't leave bruises but reshapes your soul.

I was sexually assaulted—twice—during that first tour. The pain was suffocating, but I turned it into purpose. I became a Sexual Assault Prevention and Response advocate, using my voice to protect others when I hadn't been protected.

Sometimes I still wonder if I have the right to call it what it was. Sexual assault. Because we were both drunk. Because I was underage. Because I can't remember every detail, flashes. A shower. A bed. A fog I couldn't shake. It happened at a command holiday party, one of those nights that starts with laughter and ends in a silence that follows you for years. I remember walking into the room. I remember the bottles. I remember trying to keep up, wanting to be included, not wanting to seem "too young" or "too weak."

I remember how the night spiraled, the drinks blurring the edges of my reality. Then I was in a shower with him. Then I wasn't. Then I was waking up in a bed, still wet, still hazy, still not understanding what had happened. I didn't even know how I got there. What I remember, what I will never forget, is the feeling afterward. The whispers. The looks. The comments. People looked at me sideways but never asked me if I was okay. The way they talked about me made it seem like I had asked for it. The way that I started to believe that maybe I had.

So, I went quiet. I folded into myself. I buried it deep. I didn't want to be "that girl" because I was new to the Navy. Because I didn't want to lose everything I had worked so hard to build. And because no one had ever taught me that my voice mattered, especially when it trembled. It takes me years to say it aloud. To say what happened wasn't okay.

Even if I was drinking. Even if I can't remember everything. Even if I didn't scream or fight or run. Even if part of me wanted to be seen, accepted, or liked, that doesn't make it my fault. And it doesn't make it not real. This was the first time I felt completely erased in a room full of people who smiled in my face the next day. The first time I realized how fast people will label a hurting woman instead of helping her. The first time I learned that silence is sometimes the only way women can survive in male-dominated spaces. After that night, something inside me changed.

Not immediately. Not loud. But gradually…like a dimming. Like my light didn't feel safe anymore.

I still showed up to work. Still smiled. Still did my job. But inside, I wasn't all there. I started questioning myself more than anyone else ever could. Was it my fault? Did I give the wrong impression? Did I drink too much? Was I supposed to scream? Why can't I remember? The thing about trauma is it doesn't always shout, it whispers. It sneaks in through the cracks and takes root in your self-worth. It makes you shrink in rooms you used to stand tall in, and that's what I did. I shrank. I stopped raising my hand as much. Stopped laughing as freely. I stopped trusting the air in the room because I no longer trusted myself. I buried it under the same armor I'd worn most of my life. "Be strong. Keep it together. Don't let anyone see you break." But I was breaking.

On the inside, I was grieving a version of myself that no longer felt safe in her skin. I felt dirty. Not physically. Spiritually. Emotionally. I was stained by something I couldn't scrub off, no matter how many times I wore my white dress with pride. And worse, no one knew. No one asked. No one checked in, because I didn't say anything. Because I couldn't. How do you explain to people that something happened to you when you can barely explain it to yourself? Back then, silence felt safer than the truth. But silence has a cost; it devours your voice one doubt at a time. That moment became a turning point in ways I didn't recognize until much later. I started carrying shame that didn't belong to me. Started tolerating behavior I would have once called out. Started believing I had to work twice as hard to be seen as anything other than "that girl." And just as I started to convince myself I had moved past it, it happened again. This time was different. There was no alcohol. No late-night chaos. No blurred memories or rumors filling in the gaps.

This time, it was clear and that clarity cut even deeper because this time, it was someone I trusted. He was my friend. Someone I confided in; someone who had seen the weight I carried and never judged it. He wasn't just a name in my contacts, he was someone I thought was safe. So, I agreed when he asked if he could practice on me, saying he was trying to get his massage certification. I wanted to support him. I had never even had a professional massage before. It seemed harmless. Helpful even. How stupid of me to believe that. But how could I have known? When I arrived, everything was set up as he had said. The table. The candles. The oils. The atmosphere felt calm…professional, even.

He told me to remove my top, saying it was necessary for the back massage. I kept my bra on. I still felt slightly cautious, but I brushed it off. I lay down. The massage began like I thought it would. Then, he asked me to remove my pants. Said it was going to be a "full body" now. There was a pause—a hesitation in me. But I didn't want to offend him or seem ungrateful. I told myself, this is probably normal. I told myself, you're just overthinking it. So, I said OKAY. Then I changed.

Before I could process what was happening, I felt his mouth. On my body. In places that were never offered to him. Places I never permitted him to touch. Not with his hands. And not with his mouth. I froze. My whole body tensed. My ears rang in that silence, like the world had narrowed down to my heartbeat and shame. It was like I left my body in that moment. Couldn't move. Couldn't breathe. And then it was over. I got up. Got dressed as fast as I could. Didn't say a word. Didn't even look him in the face. I just left. I never spoke to him again. But the silence inside me? That lingered. It echoed with blame. With shame. With anger at myself. Because I let him in, because I trusted him.

A part of me still questioned whether I was overreacting. But I wasn't. What he did wasn't about misunderstanding- it was about manipulation. He planned it. He set the scene. He used my trust as his weapon. He used my kindness as a gateway to violate me. That day taught me that predators don't always look like danger. Sometimes they wear the face of a friend. Sometimes they come offering help. Sometimes they say "relax" when they mean don't resist. And that moment changed me. Not just in my body. But in how I give access to my peace. How I guard my softness. How I protect the sacredness of my space. I didn't report it. I didn't scream. I didn't fight.

I realized then that not all battles are fought out loud; the hardest ones you carry inside, the ones no one claps for, but that nearly break you all the same. Some are won in the silence of deciding who you refuse to become.

But that doesn't mean I consented. Freezing is a trauma response. And now I know that too. He took something that day, but didn't take all of me. Even in the silence, I kept surviving. And now, I'm done being silent. And no one prepares you for what that does to your mind, your spirit. It shakes your sense of safety. It makes you question everything—your worth, voice, and place. I didn't crumble on the outside. I still showed up every day. I still ranked up. But I was carrying a silent weight. The kind that doesn't show up on evals. The kind that doesn't fade easily. But I refused to let it break me. Instead, I took my pain and transformed it into purpose. I became a SAPR (Sexual Assault Prevention and Response) advocate. Not because I had all the answers. But because I knew what it felt like to be voiceless. I knew what it felt like to scream silently and be met with indifference. So, I chose to be the voice I needed. I chose to sit with survivors in their broken moments so they wouldn't feel alone like I once did. I chose to believe them, support them, and fight for them, because no one fought for me. And in doing so, I started to fight for myself.

Being a SAPR advocate wasn't just about helping others and reclaiming myself. Every story I heard reminded me that I wasn't crazy. That I wasn't alone. That what happened to me mattered. It validated the brokenness I had buried so deep. And little by little, I found strength in my scars. I stopped carrying shame. I started setting firm boundaries. I began protecting my peace as if it were sacred, because it is. I started speaking up in rooms where I once stayed quiet.

I no longer needed anyone's permission to take up space. My voice, once cracked and cautious, became grounded and clear. And every time I showed up for someone else, I showed up more for myself. I realized that healing doesn't mean forgetting. It means owning the truth. It means taking back the pen and writing your story, not as a victim, but as a warrior. My advocacy, my career, my growth, it all became the proof that my trauma didn't win. I did. And now, when I look back at the girl who froze, questioned herself, and though no one would believe her…I don't feel shame. I feel pride because she didn't disappear.

She fought her way back. And she became me. Determined to be a voice for others when I had struggled to find mine. I didn't want another

Sailor to feel as alone as I did. I knew that if I could help just one person feel seen, heard, and believed, the fight would be worth it. That first chapter of my naval career was a crash course in strength. Not just physical, not just professional—but emotional, spiritual, and moral. I learned how to hold my head high in the face of injustice. I learned that silence doesn't mean weakness, but when you do find the courage to speak, it's revolutionary.

I learned that success doesn't mean the absence of scars; it means refusing to be defined by them. I left VAW-116 with two Navy Achievement Medals, a stronger backbone, and the grit you can't earn without weathering serious storms. My next stop was Commander Patrol and Reconnaissance Wing Eleven—staff duty. A completely different environment, but my mindset remained the same: show up, stand out, stay focused. From the moment I checked in, I threw myself into the mission. I worked my way to being the #1 Sailor in my department. I became known not just for getting the job done—but for doing it with precision, passion, and consistency. But it wasn't smooth sailing. The leadership I encountered early on at this command was toxic. It could've easily broken my spirit or made me retreat.

By now, I had learned how to survive under pressure—and more than that, I had learned how to thrive despite it. By then, I had become both armor and anchor for others, steady, reliable, even as I was rebuilding myself piece by piece. During this tour, I met the man who would become my husband—and my daughter's father. Life got real, real fast. I was balancing a demanding command with the shifting reality of being pregnant and stepping into motherhood. But I never let my standards slip. I still came to work as my best self. I still led. I still poured into others, even as I learned to pour into myself as a mother. I remember one moment vividly—my AO (Admin Officer) sat me down and asked, "What do you want to do with your career? "At the time, I wasn't sure. I was still figuring it out. Still piecing myself back together from everything I'd been through. But he looked at me and said, "You're going to make a great officer one day. When you're ready, let me know—I'll help you write your package." I laughed then, not knowing how prophetic his words would turn out to be. I had people in my corner who believed in me even when I didn't fully believe in myself. My Career Counselor and Command Master Chief were instrumental in helping me shape my next steps. They told me it wouldn't be easy, but it would be worth it. And they were right. I wasn't just working a job—I was building a legacy.

I was vice president of Morale, Welfare, and Recreation (MWR). I continued my work as a SAPR advocate, walking others through their pain while learning to manage my own. And despite all the personal transitions, I rose once again—this time earning Junior Sailor of the Year and walking away with a 5.0 eval. That command didn't just challenge me—it elevated me.

I left not just more decorated, but more decisive. The vision for my future was becoming clearer, and the confidence to pursue it was taking root. I had proven that no matter the weight I carried—at home, at work, within—I could still rise. And I was just getting started.

It is in the quiet that I hear my truest voice, and in that chapter of my life, it whispered, "keep going."

Chapter 7

My First Marriage

You begin to understand not only discipline, but also the sacrifices it demands—long nights on watch. The quiet weight of leadership settles on your shoulders earlier than expected—the unspoken pressure of carrying your family name in every action you take.

My reflection thinned before my resolve did. Clothes hung from me, but my spirit, quiet and stubborn, refused to disappear.

The air smelled faintly of rain, even though the sky was clear, as if the earth remembered storms I was still learning how to name. On the day we married, I tucked my doubts into the same pocket as my lip gloss.

We had been dating for about a year when I found out I was pregnant. Not long after, we got married. My marriage was supposed to be a fresh start. After years of chaos, I wanted stability, even if it didn't look like the fairy tale I once imagined. We didn't have the kind of wedding most people dream about. No aisle to walk down, no first dance, no family gathered to toast us—just the courthouse, quick signatures, and vows that felt both binding and unfinished.

By the next morning, he was back at work, and I was left in the quiet, staring at the pretty princess cut on my finger. It was a strange mix of pride and hollowness, knowing I was someone's wife but still wondering if I had really been chosen in the way I needed. The vows felt like both promise and a plea: *let this work, let me finally be chosen without having to bleed for it.*

And to be fair-he wasn't all bad.

There were moments when he showed up in ways that softened me. Sometimes I'd walk through the door and find flowers waiting on the counter. Sometimes it was a card with money slipped inside. Other times, something small-my favorite candy lay out on the dresser, like a quiet reminder that I mattered. The roses came in every color-red, pink, yellow, even white, each one saying something different when words fell short. Their scent lingered through the kitchen before I even set my bag down.

We had lighter days, too. We were gamers, and when time allowed, we'd sit side by side in front of his Xbox, hours melting away as we ran through *Grand Theft Auto* or *Left 4 Dead*. We'd pause only to order takeout or switch the screen to one of our endless horror marathons-me hiding behind a pillow, him laughing when I jumped at scenes I swore I wouldn't. We cooked together, moving around the kitchen like it was our own private dance. We carved out date nights that made it feel like we had built a small bubble where nothing outside could touch us. In those moments, it was easy to believe in us.

During my pregnancy, he showed me a gentler version of himself. He brought me whatever I craved without complaint, rubbing my feet when they swelled, bathing me tenderly, even shaving me when I couldn't manage on my own. One night, we pulled into McDonald's because I desperately wanted fries. At the speaker, he deadpanned, "Can I get a large salt-no fries?" and we laughed until we cried.

Those moments mattered. They were real. And they were exactly what made everything so complicated.

Because every kind act became a thread pulling me back in, convincing me the bad days were just a phase. One day, he made me laugh until my sides hurt. Next, he made me cry for reasons I couldn't explain without apologizing. I found myself saying sorry for things I hadn't done just to keep the peace. That tug-of-war carved confusion into me. I clung to the lighter days so tightly that I ignored how heavy the darker ones had become.

Even while pregnant, fear lived quietly beneath the hope. If he could disappear emotionally so quickly now, what would happen once our child arrived? I laughed with him, felt grateful for his car, and still, I braced myself for when it would end.

The hardest truth was realizing the good wasn't enough to erase the bad. Love without consistency is like living in a half-built house. You can paint the walls and decorate the porch, but without a roof, the storm always finds its way in. For a long time, I convinced myself that being loved sometimes was better than not being loved at all. But real love stays. It steadies. It doesn't ask you to gamble your peace on which version of someone will walk through the door.

The red flags didn't start after we were married-they were there while we were dating. Messages to other women. Conversations on his computer that crossed boundaries. I tried to rationalize it-his insecurity, his frustration, his silence. I tried to understand him. Meanwhile, I was the one breaking quietly behind closed doors.

Then I got pregnant. Then we got married. Then I had to move across the country for my career. I tried to hold everything together-the marriage, the baby, the military. But no one person can carry a marriage alone. I gave him everything I had, and it still wasn't enough to make him show up the way we needed.

After our daughter was born, the unraveling became visible. I had her at 178 pounds. A few months later, I was 120. Then 110. My collarbones sharpened. My ribs showed. I was disappearing in plain sight-physically and spiritually. And still, I stayed. I didn't want to be another failed story. I didn't want to break my family. But staying wasn't saving anyone. It was destroying me.

Jealousy, control, and resentment followed. Instead of growing up, he grew bitter. I became the mirror he couldn't stand to look into, because I reminded him of everything he hadn't done, and everything I still carried. I thought that kind of pain was normal.

We tried therapy. Advice from everyone. Family, friends, strangers. Too many voices. Not enough truth. Eventually, he asked for a divorce. I begged him to reconsider. We tried again. It got worse.

So I filed.

He tried to keep our daughter from me. Tried to sabotage my career. I fought back. I got my daughter. I started therapy. And for the first time, I chose myself, not because it was easy, but because I stopped bleeding for someone who kept handing me the knife.

And still, my pregnancy had been one of the sweetest seasons. That's the paradox. Care and neglect. Flowers and silence. Laughter and loneliness. Holding both truths is what finally taught me what kind of love I deserved,

Walking away didn't make me free. It made me face myself. And in doing so, I learned that loving someone and losing them can both be forms of freedom.

CHAPTER 8

A DAUGHTER WATCHING

After learning to walk away from what hurt me, I had to face what my choices had passed down.

She was angry, distant, and acting out in ways that didn't make sense at first. School became harder for her, and emails from teachers started piling up, concerns about behavior, focus, and emotional withdrawal. At home, the atmosphere told its own story. Dinner felt like sitting in a room full of ghosts. I pushed food around my plate while she sat across from me, arms crossed, eyes fixed anywhere but my face. Doors slammed. Footsteps stomped. Silence settled in and stayed. Even when the television was on, or the house appeared calm, tension hung thick in the air, heavy enough to press against our chests. She didn't need words to know something was wrong. She could feel it in the space between us.

I couldn't ignore it anymore.

One evening, I watched her unravel over something small-anger spilling out fast and sharp-and suddenly it hit me: she wasn't just angry at the world. She was angry at me.

It felt like watching a mirror crack open. The way her eyes glossed over with tears she refused to let fall. The way her jaw clenched, holding back words too heavy to say out loud. I had worn that same expression as a child. I saw myself in her silence, in her slammed doors, in the way she withdrew when she didn't know how to be heard. She was living out loud the frustration I had once swallowed whole, and the realization broke me.

She wasn't reacting to anything. She was responding to the life I had placed her in.

The relationship I was in at the time-the same one that was breaking me-was breaking her too. Everything she was feeling, everything she was acting out, traced back to choices I had made while trying to survive. She was absorbing pain I hadn't yet healed. She was echoing patterns I had stayed in too long. Somewhere inside herself, she was learning the same lessons I had learned far too young: that love is complicated, that silence can feel safer than speaking, that anger becomes a language when no one teaches you how to name your hurt.

One night, I sat on the edge of her bed and tried to talk to her. She wouldn't look at me. Her eyes stayed fixed on the wall, arms folded tightly across her chest. When I reached out, she pulled further into herself, wrapping the blanket around her like armor. The silence between us was unbearable, thicker than any argument we could have had. I wanted to tell her I understood. That I recognized her pain because I had carried it too. Instead, we sat there, two versions of the same story, desperate for connection and trapped in everything we didn't know how to say.

That moment changed something in me.

I couldn't let this be the life I showed her. I couldn't keep pretending things were fine when they weren't. She deserved more. And so did I.

Her silence scared me, not because she was quiet, but because I recognized it. I had lived inside that silence for years. Watching it take root in her made it clear that my healing was no longer optional. Every slammed door echoed memories of my own childhood, reminders of how dangerous silence becomes when it turns into survival.

That was when I decided to put her in therapy.

It wasn't an instant fix. At first, she didn't understand why she was there. She crossed her arms, avoided eye contact, and tapped her sneakers against the floor in quiet protest. I sat beside her, holding my breath, wondering if I had made the right choice. But slowly, session by session, something began to shift. A sentence turned into a story. A story turned into a tear she didn't try to hide. I watched her begin to unfold in ways I hadn't seen before.

One day, she walked out holding a drawing instead of words. It showed a storm breaking apart, dark clouds split by a small sun pushing through the corner of the page. Blue and gray crayon streaks filled the paper, lightning jagged across the sky, but there was light too. When she handed it to me, I wanted to cry. That picture said what she couldn't yet say out loud: *I believe things can change.*

Healing her while trying to heal myself was overwhelming. Some days it felt like I was drowning, trying to guide her through emotions I was still learning how to navigate myself. I was teaching her that it was safe to feel, to speak, to exist fully, while still learning how to do the same. There were nights I carried the weight of both our healing quietly, putting on my uniform in the morning and carrying on like nothing was breaking underneath.

But her presence gave me a reason to keep showing up.

One evening at dinner, she laughed at something small. The sound caught me off guard. It had been so long since I'd heard her laugh without a shadow behind it. Healing didn't arrive loudly. It slipped in through moments like that. I held onto that laugh like proof that we were both still there-still capable of joy.

Presence became our foundation. One Saturday morning, I chose not to rush through errands or check my phone. We sat together watching cartoons, her head leaning against my shoulder. The room filled with animated voices and soft laughter, and for once, I let the moment breathe. No multitasking. No fixing. Just being there. I realized then that presence doesn't require perfection, only consistency.

Therapy gave her language. Space. Safety. It allowed her to begin untangling emotions she had been carrying alone. It helped her understand that her anger wasn't wrong and that she didn't have to hold the weight of anyone else's mistakes. Watching her find her voice forced me to confront my own patterns. I stopped trying to prove my worth through work and productivity. I started rebuilding my relationship with myself slowly, intentionally.

I returned to things I had once loved. Reading. Writing. Quiet reflection. Long walks where I let my thoughts exist without judgement. Healing came in waves. Some days I felt strong and grounded. Other days, pain surfaced unexpectedly. But I learned that peace was something I deserved too.

As I healed, so did she.

Her anger softened. Light returned to her eyes. I watched her trust herself again. We talked-really talked-about emotions, boundaries, and accountability. I created a space where she didn't have to earn safety or suppress her truth. I showed her that love doesn't feel heavy. It doesn't silence you. It supports you.

Motherhood changed everything.

From the moment I became pregnant, something inside me shifted. Survival was no longer enough. I had to model what thriving looked like. Children don't just watch what we say; they absorb how we live. She carried pieces of me, my face, my mannerisms, and yes, my pain. Seeing that forced me to confront myself in ways nothing else ever had.

Now that she's older. I watch her with quiet pride. She's expressive. Bold. Unafraid to question what doesn't feel right. Where I once feared she might become me, I now see something better. She is becoming herself, and I am someone I'm proud for her to mirror.

One day, I sat on the edge of my bed, exhausted. I didn't say anything out loud. I just sighed and rubbed my forehead, trying to quiet my mind. She walked in, placed her hand gently on my arm, and said, "Mommy, are you okay? You look tired." Then she kissed my forehead.

That moment broke me and healed me all at once.

She didn't see the uniform. Or the responsibilities. Or the mask. She *saw* me. And that tenderness reflected the love I had poured into her, now returning to hold me steady.

Motherhood became my greatest teacher-and my redemption. Through her, I learned that cycles could break. That love can be redefined. That healing is possible, even when it's imperfect.

In her eyes, I began to see myself whole.

And if I wanted to protect that wholeness, hers and mine, I had to keep choosing healing, again and again.

CHAPTER 9

STILL, I RISE

Healing didn't stop at home. It followed me into every space I stepped into. While my daughter and I were rebuilding something tender and real behind closed doors, I was learning how to rise publicly in spaces that didn't always want me there. Two worlds existed at once: one where I was learning softness, and one where I had to sharpen myself to survive. Both were shaping me.

At home, healing looked quieter. It looked like laughter spilling across the floor while we redecorated her room, peeling old stickers off the walls and arguing playfully over which posters deserved to stay. We ate pizza straight from the box, surrounded by paint swatches and half-open boxes, music playing too loud as if joy needed to announce itself. It wasn't about the room. It was about the feeling of building something new side by side. It was about us becoming a team.

Some of our best moments happened in the car, with the windows down, music blasting, as we sang off-key without shame. Those rides reminded me that healing didn't always have to be heavy. Sometimes it sounded like laughter. Sometimes it looked easy. For the first time, I wasn't building a life around survival. I was building it around peace, around joy. Around choosing myself, whether alone or with someone who truly valued me.

Every choice from that point forward became more intentional. Softer. Rooted in alignment instead of fear. And as I continued to rise professionally, I knew my success wasn't just about rank or recognition. It was about becoming the woman I was always meant to be and showing my daughter what resilience actually looked like.

But while I was growing personally, a different kind of battle was unfolding at work.

I learned quickly that success isn't always met with celebration. Sometimes it's met with resistance. Jealousy. A quiet desire to remind you that you don't belong. I'll never forget walking into meetings where my ideas were brushed aside, only to be repeated minutes later by someone else and suddenly praised. Or the way certain coworkers avoided eye contact, whispering just loud enough for fragments of doubt to reach my ears. Each moment was small on its own, but together they painted a picture I couldn't ignore: my rise made people uncomfortable.

They didn't like seeing a woman, especially a woman of color, move quickly and confidently through the ranks. Conversations stopped when I entered rooms. My authority was questioned in ways that felt deliberate. Some days, the weight of it all pressed so hard against my chest that I wondered if I was imagining things. Other days, it was unmistakably real.

I remember one morning walking into a meeting and feeling the room shift, as if I had interrupted something I wasn't meant to hear. Papers shuffled too quickly. Eyes slid away from mine. A thin smile across the table told me everything I needed to know. Later that night, I sat in my car in the parking lot, forehead pressed against the steering wheel, wondering how many more times I could do this. And then I remembered: my daughter was watching. The reminder became my fuel.

I wasn't just fighting to climb. I was fighting to exist in rooms that wanted to erase me. The politics were cutthroat. Every move felt scrutinized, every mistake anticipated. But I refused to let their discomfort define my trajectory. I had survived too much already to fold now.

So I became strategic.

Late nights in my office turned preparation into armor. Every report was double-checked. Every brief was rehearsed until I could deliver it in my sleep. The glow of my computer screen often became the only light in the room as I whispered talking points under my breath, perfecting cadence and tone. Content mattered, but confidence mattered just as much. It wasn't just preparation. It was protection.

And yet, even in those high-pressure spaces, I found ways to keep joy alive. Some nights I turned long hours into something lighter, watching movies with my guys, dancing around the office between briefs, laughing over shared snacks and inside jokes. Leadership, I learned, wasn't just about results. It was about creating space for people to breathe. Those moments reminded me that strength and softness could coexist-even there.

Still, rising isn't always graceful.

There was a season where I became the very kind of leader I had once promised myself I'd never be. Rigid. Defensive. All control and no grace. Survival mode had hardened me, and I hadn't even realized it. It wasn't until my mentor pulled me aside one afternoon and told me the truth, that my team didn't want to work for me if I kept leading that way, that it finally hit me.

That conversation humbled me more than any evaluation ever could.

I realized I had allowed external chaos to shape how I showed up internally. My tone. My temper. My tunnel vision. None of it was strength-it was burnout. And if I wanted my Sailors to rise with me, I had to lead from balance, not bitterness.

Leadership, I learned, isn't about control. It's about influence.

Faith became my anchor during that time. Not performative faith, but quiet, private moments where I leaned into the only voice that never failed me. I prayed when the weight felt unbearable. Scriptures about endurance and purpose became armor I carried into each day. When I felt unseen, I trusted that my steps were still ordered, even when the path felt heavy.

There were nights I closed my door and let the tears fall, not from weakness, but release. I cried in the shower where the water could hide my sobs. I cried into pillows so my daughter wouldn't hear. I learned that strength wasn't about never breaking down. It was about choosing to rise anyway.

Eventually, something shifted. They realized I wasn't going anywhere.

What they didn't understand was that I had been rising my whole life. Out of unsafe homes. Out of relationships that tried to dim me. Out of every label that said I wasn't enough. This wasn't new. It was simply the continuation of a story I had been living all along.

Every step I took in that office was built on years of survival. I carried every version of myself with me-the little girl who hid in books, the woman who learned silence too early, the mother fighting to heal forward. Rising at work wasn't separate from my past. It was shaped by it.

Resilience isn't about never failing. It's about how many times you're willing to rise again.

And I wanted my daughter to see that clearly, not as perfection, but as honesty. That struggle isn't the end of the story. Rising is.

Every rise brought new lessons, but the greatest one was this:

My story was never about the fall.

It was always about the climb.

CHAPTER 10

LOVING THROUGH SURVIVAL

Freedom had felt good, but I wasn't used to it being so quiet. And then I met him.

At the time, it felt like fate. We were both in the military, navigating the demands of service life, long hours, constant moving, and the shared understanding that came with wearing the same uniform. There was comfort in the familiarity. In having someone who understood the lifestyle without explanation. And if I'm honest, I wanted stability so badly that I clung to the idea of him more than the reality of us. I wanted to build something. A home. A family. A version of love that felt different from everything I had grown up with.

Looking back now, I can see it clearly: I walked into that marriage wounded.

At first, he showered me with attention. He paid for things without hesitation, bought gifts just because, brought endless supplies of flowers, and covered me in compliments. It felt like I had finally found someone who saw me and wanted to pour into me. There was a peace in being chosen, but I confused being seen with being safe.

There were so many roses in those months that I started buying extra vases just to hold them all. My dresser became a small garden, filled with color and fragrance, daily reminders that someone was choosing me. He'd slip money into cards with nothing more than a simple *for you* scribbled

49

inside, and even that simplicity felt profound. Those gestures weren't just gifts; they were a salve, soothing old wounds that had told me I wasn't worthy of being loved in small, consistent ways.

For a while, I allowed myself to believe that maybe this was what stability finally looked like.

That consistency of affection wrapped around me like a blanket.

But slowly, almost without warning, it disappeared.

One day, the flowers stopped.

The gifts faded.

The compliments grew rare.

I couldn't pinpoint the exact moment it shifted, but I felt it. And as I began soaring in my own life—rising in my career, gaining confidence— the very things he once did to win me over vanished. I started wondering if my success had cost me his love.

The silence was the hardest part.

It wasn't just that the roses stopped coming or the cards no longer appeared- it was the way his words changed. Compliments that once flowed easily turned into interrogations.

Why are you dressed like that?

Where are you going?

The warmth I had once felt in his eyes hardened into suspicion. And when compliments did come, they felt sharp, laced with disdain. I'll never forget the moment he told me I should be lucky he was even complimenting me at all. It was like he had snatched back the very gift he once used to win me over.

The absence of kindness was louder than any argument. I was grieving a version of him that no longer existed.

At that point, I hadn't taken the time to know myself honestly. I hadn't faced the girl inside me who still believed love had to be earned through sacrifice. So I gave and gave, trying to hold everything together and be perfect.

In the beginning, I didn't understand my role. I thought love meant being flawless, being the best partner I could possibly be, especially because he had chosen me at a time when I wasn't whole. I carried that like a debt I had to repay. Instead of voicing concerns, I swallowed them. I minimized red flags. I made excuses for him, and for the parts of me that still felt unworthy of something real.

Silence doesn't erase feelings.

It only delays them.

Eventually, I began speaking up, slowly at first, then with more urgency. But by then, he had already built a story in his head: that my honesty was conflict, that my needs were arguments, that I wasn't his peace.

In reality, I was trying to bridge the growing gap between us.

Slowly, I began to disappear from that marriage.

Not all at once—but little by little.

My voice got quieter.

My light dimmed.

I was wearing the uniform, handling responsibilities, showing up every day—but inside, I was slipping.

Love built on broken pieces doesn't create wholeness.

It only deepens the cracks.

His drinking became the heaviest shadow over us. Nights blurred into arguments fueled by alcohol, his words sharper, his patience shorter. Layered on top of that was the tension between him and my daughter. They never quite got along, and I spent so much of my energy playing mediator—listening to one, then the other, trying to smooth edges that were already jagged.

Dinner often ended the same way.

Her plate pushed away.

His drink poured stronger.

The slam of her bedroom door.

His heavy footsteps out the back door.

I sat alone at the table, pretending the quiet wasn't tearing me apart.

My words became sharp not because I wanted them to be, but because they came too late, after I had swallowed too much for too long.

And somewhere in all of it, I stopped recognizing myself.

I was no longer just carrying my pain. I was carrying a marriage I didn't feel safe in, a version of myself I didn't recognize, and a silence that felt heavier than any argument we could have had.

There was a moment that should have stopped me sooner.

We were both on sea duty. Barely settled. Barely knowing each other in the ways that matter. And he asked me to get pregnant. I had told him from the beginning that I had goals, milestones I needed to hit before bringing another child into the world. I was fresh at my command, determined to one day commission as an Officer. Getting pregnant that early would have derailed everything I had worked for. I told him plainly: *let me cross over first. If we're still strong after that, then we can talk.* But asking me to give up my career before it had even started felt unreasonable - unfair.

Looking back, I believe a part of him wanted that derailment. He saw how determined I was. He knew I would hit every milestone I said I would. And instead of walking alongside that drive, he wanted to become the center of it.

Love isn't control, but sometimes we confuse possession for protection. I learned that difference the hard way.

I kept smiling in public. Performing at work. Meeting the standard. But at home, I was empty. I remember standing in front of the mirror one day, brushing my hair, staring at my reflection until my eyes blurred. I whispered it out loud, almost afraid to hear my own voice: *This isn't love.* And once I said it, I couldn't unsay it.

The neglect. The disrespect. The emotional manipulation. It didn't unravel all at once. It happened in layers, like peeling paint, each one revealing something I didn't want to see. I cried and was met with indifference. Or worse, blame. I found myself explaining basic needs, being heard, being valued and realizing I was begging for crumbs. Crumbs of effort. Crumbs of accountability. Crumbs of care.

Eventually, the pain outweighed the hope.

I didn't want to stay married. I wanted peace. Safety. Partnership. And when it became clear he wasn't willing to grow, I knew I had to go. Leaving wasn't easy. It meant facing judgement, shame, and the fear of starting over. But staying would have meant losing everything, especially myself.

Separation didn't free me the way I hoped. The silence that followed wasn't peaceful, it was deafening. I had poured so much of myself into holding something broken together that when it finally fell apart, I didn't know who I was outside of survival. I was grieving more than the loss of a husband; I was grieving the dream. And no one saw it, because I had mastered the art of wearing strength like armor.

That's what emotional damage does. It convinces you that somehow *you* are the problem, even when you were the one fighting to hold everything together.

Survival taught me how to endure. But intimacy requires something different. Intimacy asks for honesty, consistency, and mutual effort. We weren't intimate, we were surviving. Holding it together for appearances. For hope. For the idea of family. Our love looked strong from the outside, but inside it was fragile, built on patches instead of repair.

Eventually, I stopped pretending we were okay.

I stopped covering cracks with smiles. Stopped explaining away what hurt. There's a certain peace that comes when you stop fighting to prove something that no longer exists. By then, I wasn't chasing closure. I was craving peace.

What I didn't realize yet was that this wasn't the end of our story - not fully. There were still lessons waiting. Still, there are pieces I would try to salvage. Still, growth that needed to happen before I could finally walk away for good.

But this was the moment I stopped surviving for love and started choosing myself.

CHAPTER 11

HEALING IN THE FIRE

*H*eAling *didn't happen in straight lines; it circled back to test me.* We were still together then, trying to pretend that things were mending when they were really unraveling. It's strange how love can look like progress when you're desperate for peace. I wanted peace so badly that I kept calling it progress. This wasn't a new beginning-it was the same story falling apart in new ways. At first, he felt like a breath of fresh air, different from what I had known. He said all the right things, made all the right promises. And after everything I had been through, I wanted to believe him. I wanted something soft. Something safe. I wanted to rest.

But what I didn't realize was that I was still healing. And when you're still healing, your heart can confuse familiarity for love. Chaos can feel like home when you've lived in it too long.

There were relapses into doubt, into loneliness, into old habits of over-functioning to feel worthy. But there was also growth. Journal pages soaked with truth. Nights where I cried myself to sleep and woke up stronger. I remember one night sitting on the floor with my journal open, pages already soaked from tears. My daughter was asleep in my bed, and in the quiet, I wrote: *I don't know who I am right now, but I know this isn't the end of me.* That single line became my anchor, proof that even in my lowest moments, I believed in a future version of me who would rise.

Those nights with my journal weren't just writing; they were survival. I remember gripping the pen so tightly my hand shook, ink smudging as tears fell onto the page. The house was silent except for my daughter's soft breathing in the other room. I sat there afraid of tomorrow but determined not to give up. The journal became my confidant, the one place I didn't have to be strong or put together. Every messy line felt like exhaling the weight I carried all day long.

These were days when I chose myself over people, expectations, and comfort. And in the middle of it all… I was still showing up.

I was still parenting, leading, making rank, and pushing forward in my career, even as my heart was shattered. That's the part people don't always see—how women like me carry pain and progress in the same hands, how we break and still build. I learned how to mask my pain with performance. At work, I stood tall in uniform, giving orders with confidence, but inside I felt like I was crumbling. There were days I locked myself in the bathroom for just a moment of quiet, splashed cold water on my face, and then walked back out as if nothing had cracked me. At home, I smiled through homework checks and dinner prep, even when my heart was still bleeding. That was the aftermath, shattered in private, unbreakable in public, and both versions of me were real.

I started writing affirmations on sticky notes on the mirror, on the fridge, even in my daughter's lunchbox. "*We are enough.*" "Peace lives here now." They may have looked like scraps of paper, but to me, they were lifelines. Over time, those words shifted the atmosphere in our home. Less about what was broken, more about what we were building together. A slow, intentional rebuild of a woman who no longer needed saving, because she was finally learning how to save herself.

The first time I went to the gym alone after we separated, I felt awkward and exposed. But somewhere between the weights clanging and the rhythm of my breath, I realized I was building more than muscle. Every rep was a declaration: *I am still here. I am still mine.*

But healing has a way of circling back to test you. He never really left my life, and it felt like we kept restarting the same chapter, hoping for a different ending. The fights became louder than the laughter, not just with me, but with my daughter. He could be cold, dismissive, or even cruel. I tried to shield her, but children feel everything. They absorb the silence between words. I watched the light in her begin to dim the same way mine once had.

That's when I realized this wasn't just about me.

I saw my pain reflected in her eyes. Her anger. Her outburst at school. The way she withdrew. She was becoming who I once was-a little girl absorbing emotional damage she didn't ask for, learning to perform strength instead of feeling safe. I had protected everyone else for so long that I forgot to protect her. In failing to defend her, I had failed to defend myself.

Still, I kept moving forward. I threw myself into my work because it was the one place I could control the outcome. From E5 to E7, and then selected for O1E-all within the same command. We were still together then. My growth didn't inspire him; it threatened him. The more I advanced, the more it hurt his ego, his sense of identity. Instead of celebrating my wins, he resented them. The distance between us grew, subtle at first, then undeniable.

What I didn't understand then was that this wasn't new pain-it was familiar pain resurfacing. Old habits we thought we had healed returned under pressure. Patterns repeated themselves in quieter, more dangerous ways. And I was once again giving pieces of myself away to keep someone else from feeling small.

At work, I was unstoppable. At home, I was fighting a battle I was never meant to fight. My daughter felt the shift. She saw my absence, my exhaustion, my divided attention. I could see the cracks forming in her, the same ones I carried from childhood. That was the turning point.

I had to face the truth; I couldn't keep sacrificing her well-being for a life that wasn't working. I couldn't let her grow up thinking tension, silence, and resentment were normal. She deserved more. And so did I.

I ended it not just for me, but for her.

Grief didn't disappear when I left, it just changed shape. There's a photo of me from that season, hair pulled back, smile small but genuine. When I look at it now, I see someone in mid-rise. Not fully healed, but no longer broken. A woman piecing herself back together, one honest step at a time.

CHAPTER 12

REDEFINING LOVE

My career continued to advance even as I worked to rebuild my personal life. On the outside, it looked like momentum, rank, recognition, and forward motion. On the inside, it was survival paired with intention. I was learning how to keep going without abandoning myself in the process.

The highlight of that advancement came on the day of my commissioning ceremony.

That morning should have been filled only with excitement. I was giddy from the moment I woke up, smiling before my feet even touched the floor. This was my day, a milestone I had worked years for, one I had earned through grit, discipline, and perseverance. It was supposed to be pure joy.

Instead, the morning began with tension. With excuses. With that familiar heaviness that settles in when you realize you will once again have to carry the moment yourself.

There was no help with preparations. No reassurance. No quiet steadiness to lean into. I paid for everything. Planned everything. Held everything together. And for a split second, I wanted to cry not from sadness, but from exhaustion. The kind that comes from always being the strong one, even on days meant to celebrate you.

But I refused to let disappointment take this moment from me.

I pushed it down, smoothed my uniform, and stepped forward anyway because I had learned how to show up even when my world was cracking quietly beneath the surface.

When the ceremony began, I smiled for the cameras, shook hands, and stood tall as leaders and shipmates gathered to honor me. On the outside, it looked seamless. Controlled. Confident. But inside, I was still stitching myself together, reminding my heart to stay present.

Then came the moment that changed everything.

My daughter stepped forward and placed my cover on my head.

Her small hands adjusting it felt like a declaration-not just of rank, but of purpose. In that instant, the ceremony stopped being about what was missing and became about what was solid. The pride in her eyes erased the sting of the morning. Her presence reminded me why I had fought so hard to get here, not just for myself, but to show her what resilience looks like when life doesn't play fair.

Validation from others could never replace that moment. Standing there, I realized that strength doesn't mean perfection. It means showing up anyway. It means choosing yourself even when the support you hoped for doesn't arrive. It felt like two separate journeys unfolding simultaneously: one in the emotional and personal, the other professional. On the outside, it looked like I had it all together. I smiled for the cameras, shook hands, and stood tall as if nothing had gone wrong that morning. People saw confidence and control.

That day marked two journeys unfolding at once: one professional, one deeply personal.

I kept pushing forward, driven by momentum and clarity. I was reaching milestones I had once only imagined. Promotions followed. Responsibilities grew. And with each step, I learned something new about myself: I was capable of far more than I had ever believed.

For the first time, I wasn't rising out of fear or survival. I was rising because I wanted to see who I could become.

At the same time, my relationship with my daughter continued to deepen. We grew closer, more honest, more connected. I made it a point to show her, through words and actions, that her worth was not tied to anyone else's approval. Those boundaries were not selfish. That protecting your peace was not a weakness.

Watching her mirror my healing reminded me that children learn not just from what we say, but from how we choose ourselves.

As my career flourished, I knew something else had to change, too: the way I defined love.

For most of my life, I had believed love meant endurance. Staying. Fixing. Over-functioning. Carrying the weight so others didn't have to. But clarity was teaching me something different.. Real love starts with peace. With mutual presence. With choosing yourself without guilt.

The first time I said "no" without justification, it felt both terrifying and freeing. My old self would have shrunk, bent, and over-explained. This time, I simply walked away. That "no" became one of the loudest declarations of self-love I had ever made.

I learned I was worthy of respect, partnership, and support, not because of what I gave, but because of who I was. And I decided that anyone who couldn't meet me where I stood no longer had access to my life.

There were moments I felt selfish for choosing myself. For slowing down. For prioritizing healing. But I realized I couldn't teach my daughter self-worth if I continued abandoning my own. Healing isn't linear; it moves in waves. Some days, I felt grounded and whole. Other days, I felt like I was rebuilding from scratch, learning how to live honestly with the pieces.

I had to allow myself to be imperfect in front of her. To admit I didn't have all the answers. To show her that strength doesn't mean having it all together-it means being honest when you don't. To take breaks, to feel my emotions without judging myself. I also learned that healing isn't a solo journey. I couldn't do it alone, and neither could my daughter. We leaned on each other. Sometimes, she comforted me as much as I comforted her. We became partners in our healing, understanding that we could lift each other without pretending we had it all together. The space we created for each other to feel, to be vulnerable, to struggle—was sacred. Through all the pain, I also learned there's power in choosing love over fear. It wasn't just about surviving anymore—it was about truly living. I wanted my daughter to see that we could rise even when life knocked us down. And in that rise, there was strength. There was love. There was hope. Even during all the chaos and pain, I kept going. I was healing. I was mothering. I was breaking old cycles.

At the same time, I continued climbing.

I picked up Chief. I commissioned as an officer. I worked toward my bachelor's in psychology. People saw the uniform, the rank, the accomplishments—but they didn't see the nights I cried quietly, the mornings I forced myself out of bed with swollen eyes, or the weight of motherhood, healing, and ambition resting on my shoulders all at once.

At my commissioning, the shoulder boards were being placed on me. For a moment, the room blurred/ The applause faded into a distant hum. I thought of the nights I almost gave up. The moments I was told my ambition was too much. The battles no one else saw.

In that moment, I wasn't just wearing a new rank. I was carrying proof that every sacrifice, every tear, every act of endurance led me here.

And yet, I also knew rank alone wouldn't heal me.

That realization is what led me to psychology.

After everything I had been through—childhood wounds, toxic relationships, motherhood, survival—I wanted to understand the *why*. Why do we hurt? Why do we stay? Why do we shrink? Why do we survive? And how we still manage to grow.

Studying psychology became a mirror. Each class peeled back another layer of myself. I wasn't just learning about trauma and attachment—I was naming my own. And in naming it, I reclaimed power over it.

One night, while writing a paper on attachment, I paused and realized I wasn't just completing an assignment. I was writing my way back to myself.

When my daughter hugged me and said, "Mom, you're going to help people," I knew she saw me, not just as her mother, but as a woman becoming.

Everything I had lived through began to make sense, not as punishment, but as preparation.

Redefining love meant understanding that what I gave myself mattered just as much as what I once sought from others. It meant building a life anchored in peace, purpose, and presence. It meant choosing not to abandon myself ever again.

Everything I've been through can be used to help someone else one day. Those may be the most broken parts of my life, but they are the pieces that will allow me to help others heal, too. I didn't go through all this just to survive it. I believe my story, my pain, healing, and growth were meant to be used. I want to be the person I needed when I was younger. I want to be a safe place for those who feel unseen, unheard, and unloved because I know exactly what that feels like.

Looking back, the ceremony was never just about promotion. It was about permission to stand tall, to let go, and to love myself differently.

And that became the foundation on which I built everything else.

Chapter 13

⁓

Mother. Leader. Survivor.

With my degree in psychology, I plan to do more than work—I want to impact. After everything I'd endured, I no longer saw just a title on a diploma – I saw evidence of endurance, faith, and follow-through. I picture a circle of women gathered in a safe space, shoulders softening as they finally let go of what they've carried. I can already see myself in those rooms, standing at the front, not as someone untouchable, but as someone who has walked through the fire and made it out alive. I would start not with lectures, but with presence. I'd look each woman in the eye and remind her that she is not invisible, that her pain has a place here, but so does her healing. I'd share pieces of my story, not as a blueprint, but as proof that brokenness and brilliance can exist in the same body. My goal wouldn't be to fix them; it would be to help them remember that they were never truly broken to begin with. The chairs are comfortable, the lighting warm, and the air hums with honesty. Some voices tremble, some rise bold and unashamed, but all are heard. In that room, healing doesn't just feel possible, it feels invisible.

This is more than a career. This is my calling. Through it all, I remained grounded in my belief that my career was part of a greater purpose. I wasn't just fighting for a position; I was fighting for something more profound. It wasn't just about climbing the ranks—it was about showing my daughter, and anyone else watching, that success isn't handed to you. You must fight for it, earn it, and stay true to who you are, even when the world around you is trying to tear you down. Ultimately, I became the person I had always dreamed of being in my career and life. I learned that promotions or titles don't just measure true success—it's measured by the ability to persevere, to stay aligned with your values, and to remain steadfast in the face of adversity. And I carried my daughter's future with me every step of the way. She had to see that no matter how hard it got, you never stop fighting for what's yours. Personal growth didn't come easily. It was born out of pain, built through perseverance, and sharpened by every trial I had to overcome. But once it took root, it changed everything. I began to see myself differently. Where I once felt like I had to prove my worth to be seen constantly, I started realizing that I was enough—even when no one else acknowledged it. I stopped searching for validation from others because I had finally found it within myself. The girl who used to hide behind perfection, behind books, behind accomplishments, started to step into the light. I wasn't perfect, but I was powerful. I wasn't just surviving anymore—I was becoming. I learned that boundaries are a form of self-respect. For years, I let people take and take—my time, my energy, my peace—because I thought that's what it meant to be strong. But real strength meant saying no. It meant walking away from people who weren't healthy for me, even when it hurt. It meant holding others accountable, not just for how they treated me, but for their impact on my daughter, my future, and the peace I was trying to build. I began to prioritize my healing.

That looked like therapy, prayer, quiet time, and journaling. Healing required discipline, the kind that made me choose stillness over distraction. There were mornings when I rose before the sun, the house quiet except for the hum of the refrigerator. With coffee steaming in my cup and my journal open, I poured myself on the page. The scratch of the pen against paper became its own kind of release, my prayers woven into every word. Other nights I worked by lamplight, exhaustion heavy, but my determination heavier.

There were mornings I sat in silence with my bible open, not even reading at first, just breathing. Slowly, the words became prayers, the prayers became habits, and the habits became healing. Those small, quiet rituals built the woman I am today more than any title ever did.

Whatever it took to unlearn the lies I'd been told and start speaking truth over my life. That decision became the quiet revolution inside of me. I realized I had been carrying the weight of other people's pain for far too long. Their opinions, their limitations, their dysfunction—it had shaped how I saw myself. But I wasn't that little girl anymore. I was evolving. Motherhood became my mirror. Every step I took toward healing was reflected in my daughter. When I showed her grace, I learned to offer it to myself. When I apologized to her, I taught myself that growth doesn't require shame. When I protected her, I was finally protecting the little girl in me who never got that same care. Raising her while rebuilding myself forced me to become intentional in every area of life—how I spoke, loved, and lived. I'll never forget the day my daughter caught me laughing again, really laughing. It was such a small moment: we were sitting at the table eating dinner, and she said something silly, and instead of brushing it off with the half-smiles I had grown used to, I laughed so hard that tears welled up in my eyes. She froze for a second, wide-eyed, and then smiled as if she'd been waiting for that sound. It was in that instant that I realized how much she had been watching me, silently measuring her world by my energy. My healing wasn't just for me; it was a mirror she looked into every single day. My voice got stronger.

I stopped shrinking to make others comfortable. That shift changed everything, not just how I showed up in rooms, but how I showed up at home. My daughter started to notice too, she'd say, "Mom, you don't let people talk over you anymore. "Another time, she told me, 'Mom, you laugh more now, you don't look so tired anymore.' Her words caught me off guard, because she saw in me what I hadn't yet named for myself. Healing wasn't just something I carried on the inside; it was written on my face, visible to the one watching me closest. That was proof that my healing wasn't just mine, it was hers too.

By the time new opportunities arrived, I was no longer a woman waiting for permission.

The first time I stood in a room full of people and spoke my truth. I remember the silence right before my words filled the air, the pounding of my heart echoing in my ears. For a split second, I doubted myself. Would my voice shake? Would anyone even care? But when I spoke, the sound was strong, steady, and it surprised me. The more I talked, the more the room leaned in, as if my truth gave others permission to breathe deeper, to uncover pieces of their own courage. I felt my voice vibrate differently. I wasn't asking permission anymore. I wasn't softening the truth to make it palatable. I was fully present, and for the first time, I realized this is what power feels like when it's rooted in peace. I learned to stand in rooms where I once felt I didn't belong—and speak as if I owned the space, not out of arrogance but out of awareness. I had worked too hard to play small. Every version of me that survived before this deserved to be honored.

The girl who escaped through books. The young woman who endured abuse. The mother who gave her daughter what she never had. The leader who rose through the ranks despite the opposition. They were all pieces of the woman I am now—a woman who doesn't just hope for better but creates it. Everything I went through—every heartbreak, betrayal, and silent tear cried behind closed doors—was preparing me. I didn't know it then, but each storm shaped me into a woman who could survive and build. I'm no longer living on autopilot or just going through the motions. I'm intentional. Every move I make, every decision I choose, is rooted in peace, purpose, and alignment. I'm not just reacting to life—I'm creating it. I finally know what I want and, more importantly, what I deserve. I won't settle for less, not in love, not in friendship, not in career, and not within myself. I've learned how to protect my space. Not everyone gets access to me anymore. I used to let people stay in my life out of loyalty, fear, and habit—but now, I choose peace over people-pleasing. I no longer carry what isn't mine. And if someone threatens the stability I've worked so hard to build—for myself or my daughter—I don't hesitate to let them go. That's not cold. That's growth.

I'm building a life where my daughter can thrive and feel safe. She gets to see what it looks like to heal and still rise. She grows up knowing she's seen, heard, and deeply loved—not just by me, but by the woman I'm becoming. Every decision I make now has her in mind. I'm breaking cycles. I'm building bridges. I'm showing her that being soft and firm can coexist—that she can be powerful without losing her kindness. The life I'm building now is rooted in truth.

I'm not hiding anymore. Not behind achievements. Not behind resilience. Not behind survival. I'm embracing softness, slowing down, listening to my intuition, and permitting myself to rest. To breathe. To receive. That's a different kind of strength I had to earn through fire.

And even though life still throws challenges my way, I'm not the same woman who used to question her worth.

Now, I walk in confidence. Not because life is perfect—but because I finally am. Not flawless, not finished, but whole in a way I never knew was possible.

I'm building a life that reflects who I am:

Grounded. Purposeful. Free.

Still healing, but no longer breaking.

For the first time, I see the black sheep not as a curse; it felt like a crown, bold, unmistakable, and wholly mine. For years, I tried to blend in, to dim my light so others would feel comfortable. But now, standing apart felt regal, like carrying a fire only I could tend. Being the black sheep didn't isolate me anymore; it set me apart with purpose.

Wearing the black sheep crown no longer feels like exile; it feels like an inheritance. What once made me feel cast out has become the very thing that sets me apart as a leader, a mother, and a survivor. I carry it proudly now, not just for myself, but as a torch for my daughter and for every woman who has ever been told she was "too much" or "not enough." If this is the crown I was meant to wear, then I will wear it boldly, knowing it shines brightest in the places others once tried to dim me.

CHAPTER 14

MOTHERING THROUGH THE FIRE

I have learned that children do not miss a thing.

They carry our moods like mirrors, reflecting even what we try to hide. My daughter saw everything: the fights, the sadness, the silence that lingered after arguments.

Sometimes she didn't say a word, but her silence screamed at me louder than any tantrum could have. At dinner, she would sit across from me, fork hovering over her plate, pretending to eat. Her eyes followed me carefully, like she was taking notes, like every sigh and every tired glance carried a secret message only she could decode. Her silence at the table cut deeper than any words could. I would sit across from her, pushing food around my plate, wishing I could find the right thing to say to ease the weight she carried. But all I managed most nights was a tired smile or a half-hearted attempt at small talk. Inside, I wanted to reach across the table, grab her hands, and tell her I understood that I was trying. Instead, I held myself together, keeping my posture straight, my face unreadable, knowing my body language probably spoke louder than my words. She was studying me, and I knew it, but sometimes I feared the lesson she was learning was how to suffer quietly. The TV might be blaring cartoons in the background, but she wasn't laughing the way other kids did. Instead, she sat curled up on the couch with her knees pulled to her chest, staring at me as though she was trying to figure out if I was okay. In those moments,

I realized she was doing the very thing I had done as a child—monitoring the adults in the room, adjusting her emotions to match the temperature. That realization gutted me. There were nights when she disappeared into her room and closed the door without a word. I would stand outside, listening for movement, waiting for some sound to let me know she was okay. Sometimes I heard muffled crying, other times nothing at all, and the silence was worse. I wanted to knock, to push the door open and promise her that it would all get better, but shame kept my hand frozen at my side. I hated that my daughter's safe place had become an escape from me and the chaos I couldn't shield her from.

The calls from school, the sleepless nights, the frustration—it all weighed on her small shoulders. She often overheard the late-night arguments, even when I thought she was asleep. I would find her the next morning, eyes tired, asking in a small voice, "is everything okay now?" Those words cut me deeper than the fights themselves, because she shouldn't have been carrying the weight of reconciliation.

I saw the same weary hope I once carried as a little girl, waiting for peace that never came.

She should have been dreaming about dolls and school projects, not wondering if her world would still be standing when she woke up.

Each phone call from the school carried a weight I can still feel today. The ring itself became a trigger, tightening my chest before I even picked up. On the other end, the teacher's voice was always polite but strained, a mix of concern and exhaustion. Hearing my daughter's name tied to words like "disruptive," "withdrawn," or "unfocused" made me want to scream that she wasn't a problem—she was a little girl carrying burdens too heavy for her age. But instead, I swallowed my explanations, thanked them for letting me know, and hung up with a lump in my throat. I carried that weight home, replaying her name mixed with judgment, vowing silently that she would not be defined by those moments. Every call from the school felt like a dagger aimed at both of us. I wanted to defend her, to tell the teachers that her behavior wasn't defiance, it was pain spilling out in ways she didn't know how to control. But instead of saying what I really felt, I bit my tongue, nodded through their concerns, and promised to "work on it at home." What I carried back with me, though, were silent vows that she would not be reduced to a checklist of problems, that her story wouldn't be defined by the red marks on her behavior chart. Those silent defenses stacked up in my chest, heavier each time, until even I had to remind myself she was more than her worst days.

She mirrored me in ways I wished she wouldn't. She masked her pain, just as I had as a little girl.

I remember watching other kids run past us one afternoon, laughing, backpacks bouncing, sunscreen still shining on their cheeks. The smell of grass and the sound of sprinklers filled the air. My daughter stood frozen, tears streaking down her face, clutching the strap of her backpack like it was her only shield. She wasn't just crying—she was pleading, silently, with her body language, for safety. That look broke me because no child should ever have to beg for the protection that should already be guaranteed.

Driving home that day, guilt pressed against my chest so hard it was difficult to breathe. I replayed her tears, her fear, her refusal, and I hated myself for not leaving sooner-for not recognizing how deep the damage had gone. I wanted to be her shield, but instead I felt like the crack in the armor, the weak spot where pain slipped through—realizing that I was the common denominator, the one trying to hold everything together while it crumbled anyway, was unbearable.

I'll never forget the day the camp counselor called me. My daughter had run into the bathroom crying, refusing to get into the car with my second husband. She said she didn't feel safe. I could hear the terror in her voice through the phone, and my heart dropped. I told her, "If you get in the car with him this one time, you will never have to get in the car with him again." My voice was steady, but inside I was breaking.

That call etched itself into me. Motherhood demanded an impossible balance-her immediate safety weighed against long-term promises. A reminder of how fragile trust can be, and how much she needed to know I would always fight for her. I thought I had protected her by staying strong, but strength without softness had built walls between us.

Therapy came next.

She folded her arms in session, unwilling to talk, holding everything in.

The waiting room always smelled faintly of disinfectant and crayons. The kind of place meant to comfort, but never quite succeeds. I sat there with my stomach in knots, the tick of the clock louder than my thoughts. When the therapist spoke to her gently, asking the simplest questions, I watched her lips stay pressed together in defiance. It took weeks before she let even a single word slip, and when she did, it felt like the smallest but most significant victory. That first word opened the door a crack, but it was weeks before she trusted the space enough to let more out.

In one session, she cried quietly, tears sliding down her cheeks as she clutched a pillow to her chest. Another time, she whispered, "I don't like when he yells," referring to my second husband, and my heart shattered at the simplicity of her truth. Each breakthrough was small, but together they built a path forward. Watching her piece herself back together was humbling, and it taught me patience in ways I'd never known before.

Those therapy sessions didn't just change her; they changed me.

Sitting in that room, I learned to slow down. To listen without defending myself. To sit with discomfort instead of rushing to fix it. Week by week, as she found her voice, I learned new ways to mother, less control, more presence. Healing wasn't something I could hand her like a wrapped gift. It was something we had to walk through together.

Some days that walk felt like crawling, but we kept moving, one breath at a time. I was determined she wouldn't become me. I wanted her to know emotions weren't weakness—they were proof of life.

One night, she caught me crying at the kitchen table, my face buried in my hands. For a moment, I thought she would run away, but instead, she walked over quietly and placed her hand on mine. We didn't speak. That simple gesture told me she needed to see that I wasn't invincible—that even moms bleed, and that it was okay to show it. Her touch that night was as much healing for me as it was for her. That moment cemented a vow in me. I swore she would never grow up questioning her worth the way I once did. She would not have to wait until adulthood to learn that her voice mattered, that her feelings were valid, and that love should never come laced with fear. If I had to be broken and rebuilt a thousand times to make sure she felt safe, I would do it without hesitation. She deserved a foundation stronger than mine, and I was determined to give it to her.

When I heard her laugh again, really laugh, it was like music. That sound wasn't just joy; it was proof the fire hadn't taken her spirit. Watching her rebuild gave me permission to keep rebuilding, too. In saving her, I realized she had saved me as well.

CHAPTER 15

HER EYES SAW WHAT I HID

She was about eight or nine when she said it. We were in the middle of another day – just the two of us, trying to make the best of a home that had felt like a battlefield. I don't even remember what triggered the moment. But I remember asking her why she always yelled so much.

And she looked at me, so calmly, and said: Because that's what you all do, you taught me. That's how I need to be. Her words knocked the wind out of me.

It wasn't defiance, it was observation, the kind that only comes from years of watching me break and rebuild in front of her. I remember staring at her, searching her face for any sign that she didn't mean it, that maybe I had misheard. But she was calm, almost too calm for a child her age, her eyes steady in a way that felt older than her years. My stomach twisted because I realized she wasn't just repeating something she had seen once or twice; she was naming the cycle she had been raised in. It wasn't anger in her tone; it was resignation. Her eyes were steady, too steady for a child her age. There was no fire in them, only a tired knowing, the kind of wisdom that should never belong to someone so young. In that moment, I felt like I was staring into a mirror of my younger self, eyes that had seen too much, a voice too calm for the weight it carried. She looked older than she was, like she had skipped stages of innocence because life had handed her chapters she was never supposed to read. And it broke me to realize she had learned silence the same way I had by surviving. She was telling me, without even knowing it, that she had learned how to bury herself alive the same way I had.

I just stood there frozen because I realized at that moment, I hadn't just taught her survival. I had taught her how to carry my pain. She didn't know peace. She didn't know softness. She didn't know what it felt like to feel emotionally safe at home. She once told me, "There is no peace here. I want a little bit of peace."

Peace for her would have been simple, waking up without tension in the air, eating breakfast without bracing for someone's mood to explode, going to bed without hearing muffled arguments through the walls. Her idea of peace wasn't big vacations or fancy gifts. It was laughter that lasted longer than a moment, a home where safety didn't vanish when the sun went down, and the freedom to be a child without carrying the weight of grown-up battles. When she said she wanted peace, she was asking for what every child deserves, but too many go without: a home that feels like shelter, not a storm.

Her words pulled me back into my own childhood. I remembered lying awake, wishing for quiet, for safety, for a home where I didn't have to measure every breath against someone else's temper. I wanted peace then, the same way she was asking for it now. The parallel was undeniable, and it hit me with the sharpness of generational truth. What we don't heal, we repeat. And here I was, staring at the cycle playing out in my daughter's life, the very cycle I had promised myself I would break.

That crushed me.

Because all I ever wanted was to protect her, and somehow, even with all my effort, she still ended up feeling unprotected.

I used to wonder why she loved staying over at her friend's house. Why did she always linger there just a little longer than usual? Why did coming home make her mood shift so quickly?

It's because my home didn't feel safe. It felt like tension. It felt like waiting for the following argument to explode. It felt like walking on eggshells – even for her.

Every time I had to go away and leave her with my now ex-partner, it was always something. The calls always came while I was in uniform, between briefings or watches, and I'd have to swallow the helplessness before anyone saw it.

He calls me, yelling.

Get your daughter. She's not listening. I don't have time for this.

And the cruelest part?

He knew I couldn't come.

I wasn't even in town.

But he'd still say it, making her feel unwanted, like a burden.

One time, he dragged her to the front door, threatening to leave her.

Another time, he purposely made her late for practice. And when she cried in the car, he pulled into a parking lot and said, "Now you're going to be late."

She told me later how humiliated she felt sitting in the passenger seat with tears running down her cheeks. She clutched her water bottle in her lap like it was the only thing she could control. Her hands shook as she tried to wipe her face, but the more she tried to hide her tears, the harder she cried. I can still picture her small frame hunched against the car door, her body angled away as if shrinking could make her invisible. That moment didn't just make her late; it made her feel unworthy, unseen, like her pain was a joke to him. And that memory etched itself into me as one of the deepest regrets of staying too long.

He ruined birthdays, Holidays, Christmas, and Halloween. We faked it. Even laughter had become rehearsed, a performance we both knew by heart—year after year. Smile for the pictures.

I can still see the holiday table laid out with all the trimmings, the smell of fried turkey, pies cooling on the counter, the sound of laughter rising just loud enough to cover the tension. In the pictures, you see smiles and matching outfits, balloons and candles, costumes and bright wrapping paper. What the pictures don't show is how forced those smiles felt, how I would catch my daughter glancing at me when no one else was looking, her eyes begging me to admit the truth neither of us could say out loud.

The photos became proof of a lie, glossy images that told the world we were happy while inside we were unraveling. Those holidays drained me in ways no one could see. I would iron the matching outfits, cook the big meals, string the decorations, and pose for the photos with a smile I had to force through clenched teeth. Every staged laugh felt like another mask layered on top of the last, hiding the truth of how fragile we were behind closed doors. By the time the dishes were washed and the house went quiet, I was exhausted, not from the celebration itself but from the performance of pretending we were a family untouched by the cracks.

Sometimes I look back at those photos, the costumes, the candles, the forced smiles, and all I can see now is the tension hiding behind our eyes. We were living proof that pictures can lie.

The truth is, we had become experts at masking: matching outfits, matching smiles, matching silence. But underneath, both of us were unraveling. And when she finally said the words about wanting to die, it stripped every mask away. I knew then that pretending was no longer an option.

Laugh through the tension. Act like we were okay until we couldn't fake it anymore. Eventually, the cracks showed at school, too. Call after call. Behavior changes. Anger, Isolation.

Then one day, she said she wanted to kill herself. The room froze around me. I remember the way my heart dropped into my stomach, the way my hands suddenly felt cold and clammy. I couldn't even breathe at first because hearing those words from her tiny mouth felt like the ground had split beneath us both. I wanted to gather her in my arms and promise her it would never feel that way again, but the truth was, I didn't know how to fix it yet. I held her face in my hands, whispered that she mattered, that her life had meaning, even as tears blurred my own vision. In that moment, I felt both the crushing weight of failure and the burning determination that I would not lose her.

The words froze time. My chest tightened, my ears rang, and I remember clutching the counter to stay upright. I never imagined my little girl would carry that kind of weight, and it shattered me to know my choices had let it happen.

The air in the room turned heavy, like even oxygen didn't want to move. I could hear the faint hum of the refrigerator, the distant sound of traffic outside, and her small, shaking breaths. Her face was solemn, her eyes swollen from crying, and yet she looked at me with a raw honesty that stripped me bare. My hands trembled as I reached for her, every nerve in my body screaming that this was the line, there would be no going back if I didn't act now. In that split second, I told myself something had to change. Not tomorrow. Not someday. Right now.

I couldn't breathe, and I didn't understand at first. Didn't know where it was coming from. But over time, it all made sense. It was the relationship. The environment. The man I had let stay too long. The damage I thought I was shielding her from was hitting her head on.

She didn't just see what I tried to hide – she lived it, and in that realization, something in me broke open. I knew I couldn't just keep surviving; I had to choose differently, for her and for me.

That night, I made a vow that went deeper than survival. It wasn't just about saving her in the moment; it was about saving the generations after her. I refused to let her story, or mine, end in silence and repetition. I wanted her children, and their children, to inherit something different; laughter that wasn't forced, peace that wasn't borrowed, love that wasn't conditional. The cycle would stop here, with me.

CHAPTER 16

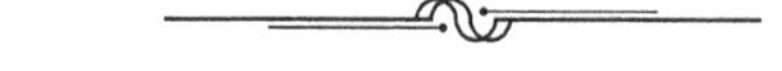

THE THERAPY CHAIR

I sat down in the chair and felt the silence press in around me, even though all I was really being asked to do was sit.

The room felt both safe and foreign at the same time. The walls were painted a soft beige, the kind of color meant to calm you, but my nerves didn't care. I noticed the faint smell of coffee, the steady tick of a clock, and a box of tissues on the side table that felt like it was daring me to break. The chair was comfortable, but I couldn't relax. I crossed and uncrossed my legs, tapped my nails against the armrest, anything to keep from sinking too far into my own silence. I felt exposed, like I had walked into battle without armor, even though all I was really being asked to do was sit.

My palms were damp against my thighs, leaving faint marks on the fabric of my pants. I kept shifting in the chair, trying to find a position that didn't make me feel like I was on display. My chest rose and fell too quickly, breaths shallow, like I couldn't quite catch enough air. Every part of me wanted to bolt, walk out the door and pretend I didn't need this, but another part of me was so exhausted from pretending that I stayed put. It felt foreign to be in a space where I was the only focus, where the question wasn't what do you need me to do? But how are you, really?

Maybe I thought I'd cry.

Or lie.

Or finally say aloud everything I'd buried.

Maybe I thought I'd finally say aloud all the things I had buried so deep I couldn't feel them anymore.

But I just sat there.

Tense. Guarded.

Not because I didn't want to be helped, but because I had spent years performing strength.

I wasn't used to being seen.

I had been the strong one—the glue.

The one who kept the schedule, handled the home, paid the bills, and made sure everyone else was okay – even when I wasn't.

At home, being the "strong one" looked like late nights folding laundry when my body was screaming for rest. It looked like I was smiling at school functions, even when I had been crying in the car minutes before. It looked like making sure bills were paid, groceries stocked, and my daughter's hair done, while my own life felt like it was unraveling thread by thread.

Nobody asked how I was doing because my role was clear: hold it all together.

I wore strength like a uniform, neat and pressed on the outside, while the inside of me was fraying.

Strength had become a performance I perfected. I laughed at jokes I didn't find funny, brushed off questions with a quick, "*I'm fine*, and kept myself busy enough to avoid silence. If I wasn't at work, I was cleaning, cooking, running errands, anything to keep from sitting still long enough to feel.

My calendar was always full, not because I wanted it to be, but because exhaustion was easier to manage than loneliness. I thought if I stayed moving, the cracks wouldn't show.

But inside, I knew the weight I carried was eating me alive.

I had been breaking in silence for so long, I forgot what it felt like to be held without condition.

My therapist asked me simple questions at first

What brought me here? What did I want to work on? What was I carrying?

I wanted to say everything. I wanted to say nothing.

Because the truth is—I didn't know where to start.

The room was quiet except for the hum of the air vent. I stared at the box of tissues on the table, willing myself not to reach for them too soon. My fingers knotted in my lap, betraying the storm inside.

How do you begin to unravel a lifetime of pain? Where do you start when the wounds are layered? When do the voices in your head sound like those who said they loved you?

I remember sitting with my very first therapist, one of the three I would eventually see, and he just looked at me, shook his head slowly, and said:

How are you still even here?

His words hung in the air heavier than any silence I had ever sat in.

No one had ever asked me that before. People saw me functioning and assumed I was fine, but here was someone looking straight at me, naming my survival as if it were a miracle. I didn't know whether to laugh, cry, or get up and walk out.

The question pierced through every layer I had built, and I felt both validated and exposed. I realized in that moment that I had been living so long in survival mode that I had never stopped to consider the toll it took just to still be breathing.

His words continued to echo in my head, pulling me back to nights I thought nobody saw. Nights when I sat in the dark, staring at the wall, wondering what it would feel like to simply stop. The moments when I smiled for others day by day, but collapsed into tears alone at night.

Survival had become my normal, always bracing for the next storm, never daring to exhale fully. To have someone name it, to have someone see it, was both terrifying and relieving.

Terrifying because it meant I couldn't keep lying to myself, relieving because maybe—just maybe—I wasn't as invisible as I thought.

Even he couldn't believe that I had carried all that pain and still showed up smiling.

And all I could say was:

"I don't know. Someone is praying harder than I'm praying for myself."

That moment stayed with me.

Because it reminded me of what I already knew deep down—that what I survived should have broken me.

But I was still standing. I kept showing up.

Week after week. Peeling back layers.

In one session, I talked about my grandmother. Another, my mother. Another, my partners.

When I talked about my grandmother, memories came in fragments-the sound of her slippers shuffling across the floor, the way she could cut with her words and then act as if nothing happened. With my mother, it was different: a complicated love, full of gaps where tenderness should have been, patched over with obligation and silence.

And when I spoke about my partners, especially the ones who left scars, I felt my voice tighten, like the words themselves were stuck in my throat. Each story felt like peeling off a bandage that had been on for too long, realizing wounds I didn't even realize were still bleeding.

And then eventually, my daughter.

And when I spoke of her, that's when the tears came.

The words stumbled out between sobs, my chest heaving like it had been holding its breath for years. I pressed the tissues hard against my face, but they couldn't keep up with the flood. It wasn't crying, it was breaking open.

The sobs came in waves, raw and uncontrollable, shaking my whole body. I remember clutching the tissue so tightly it tore my hand. My chest ached, my face burned hot, and I couldn't stop even when I wanted to.

By the time it slowed, I felt hollowed out, drained, shaky, but somehow lighter.

My therapist didn't rush to fill the silence. He just let me sit in the wreckage of it.

The silence gave me permission to breathe again. To realize that breaking open didn't mean I was weak. It meant I was finally letting myself be human.

The first time I said my daughter's name out loud in that chair, my voice cracked in a way I couldn't control. It was as if all the grief, guilt, and love I had been swallowing for years came rushing out at once.

My tears weren't just for her, they were for me, for the mother I wished I had been, for the moments I knew I had missed, for the ways I had failed in silence.

Saying her name broke something open in me, but it also planted a seed. I realized that talking about her didn't make me less strong. It made me more human, more determined to do better.

But you know what my therapist told me?

Even if you didn't have the perfect tools, you showed up. You're here. That means something.

That was the first time I permitted myself not to have it all together. To admit I was tired.

To admit I needed help. To admit I couldn't fix everyone else and heal myself in the same breath.

For the first time, I exhaled.

Therapy didn't save me. I did.

But therapy gave me a mirror. A safe place to take off the mask. A reminder that healing wasn't about being strong, it was about being real.

And from that chair, week by week, I started coming back to myself.

Therapy became a mirror I couldn't avoid. Week after week, I saw not just my pain but also my resilience staring back at me. I began to recognize the parts of myself I thought I had lost-the girl who once laughed easily, the woman who still dreamed, the mother who wanted more for her child.

Slowly, the reflection shifted from someone barely surviving to someone daring to hope.

It wasn't overnight. It wasn't easy.

But the chair became the place where I learned that my story wasn't over. It was just beginning again, this time on my terms.

Therapy didn't fix me overnight, and it wasn't a cure-all, but that chair became something sacred to me. It was the one place where I could take off the mask without fear of judgement, where my shaking hands and trembling words were enough.

Each session was another brick laid in the foundation of the woman I was becoming- strong not because she held everything in, but because she finally let it out.

Healing was slow. Messy. Imperfect.

But it was mine.

And for the first time, I believed it was worth the work it took to rebuild.

Not the woman I was, but the one I was finally ready to be.

CHAPTER 17

BUILDING A NEW WAY TO LOVE

Therapy didn't just help me process my past; it forced me to redefine what love meant.

Because the truth was, I didn't know.

I thought love was sacrifice. I thought love was staying. I thought love was holding everything together, even when it was breaking me.

I learned to associate love with struggle.

It had been my normal for so long that peace felt foreign. Peace stopped feeling like silence and started feeling like safety. I didn't know how to sit in stillness without waiting for the next storm.

There were so many times I mistook pain for proof. I told myself that staying through the arguments, forgiving the broken promises, and swallowing my own needs meant I was loyal. I believed that the more I endured, the more it proved my love was real. Red flags weren't warnings to me back then; they were challenges I thought I had to push through. A last-minute bouquet of flowers after weeks of neglect, or an apology whispered without change, I took as signs that maybe he still cared. I thought love meant tolerating, adjusting, shrinking if I had to, to keep the peace. It took therapy to teach me that real love doesn't ask you to sacrifice yourself to prove it exists.

With fixing. With being chosen only when I was useful.

89

There were times I confused chaos with passion, believing that the more I endured, the deeper the love must have been. I stayed in rooms where my voice was dismissed, telling myself that my patience was proof of loyalty. I accepted apologies that came with no change, mistaking bare minimum gestures for devotion. I called it love when I was really just surviving, stretching myself thin to keep someone else comfortable. Back then, I thought sacrifice meant proof. Now I see it was evidence of how little I believed I deserved.

But that wasn't love.

That was survival in disguise.

So, I started building a new way to love.

It started with me.

I stopped apologizing for my boundaries.

The first time I said no without over-explaining, I braced myself for backlash that never came. Instead, I felt an unfamiliar sense of peace, proof that protecting my space didn't require permission. My chest tightened as the word left my lips, simple but heavy. I waited for the explosion of anger, disappointment, or guilt to come crashing down. But instead, the air stayed still. The silence stretched, and I realized I didn't need to scramble to explain or soften the blow. My "no" stood on its own. That moment felt both terrifying and liberating. Healing demanded new habits. The first time I said "no, I felt it everywhere: my throat tightened, my hands shook, and for a split second, I thought I'd cave and take it back. But when I didn't, when the word stayed out there without explanation, something shifted inside me. I realized the world didn't end just because I stopped overextending myself. That one boundary carried over into the smallest corners of my life; saying no to a favor I didn't have time for, no to staying late at work when I was exhausted, no to family members who expected me to always be available. Each "no" added another brick to the foundation of the woman I was becoming, stronger, steadier, more unapologetic.

Boundaries became my proof of growth, not my punishment.

My body shook, my palms damp with sweat, but underneath the fear was a flicker of power. I had protected my boundary, and nothing bad happened.

Stopped minimizing my voice to make others comfortable.

Stopped showing up for people who only called me when they needed something

I started listening to my body.

Resting.

Eating.

Moving.

Caring for myself in ways I didn't even know I was allowed to before.

Sometimes self-care looked like the smallest choices, sitting with my journal and pouring my heart onto the page instead of bottling it up, cooking a meal that nourished me instead of rushing through fast food, or letting myself take a nap without guilt. Other times it was bigger: signing up for a fitness class, going for a walk to breathe in the evening air, or letting music fill the room while I danced in the kitchen with my daughter. Each act was a quiet rebellion against the version of me that once believed exhaustion was the price of love.

One evening, I remember lighting a candle, cooking my favorite meal, and dancing around the kitchen to music that made me feel alive. No one was there to see it, no one to perform for, it was just me reclaiming joy. Another night, I curled up with a blanket and journaled for hours, pouring out words that had been stuck in me for years. When I closed that notebook, I realized I hadn't felt guilty once for taking that time. Self-care wasn't about face masks or spa days for me; it was about teaching myself that rest wasn't laziness, that joy didn't have to be earned, and that I was worthy of softness even without anyone else's validation.

I was finally mothering myself the way I had always mothered everyone else.

I learned that self-love wasn't bubble baths and face masks – it was discipline.

It was choosing peace over patterns.

It was saying "no" without explaining.

It was trusting my intuition – even when it didn't make sense to anyone else.

I started loving my daughter differently, too.

Not from guilt. Not from overcompensation.

But with intention.

With listening. With softness. With truth.

I looked her in the eyes and spoke:

I'm sorry. I didn't always get it right. But I'm trying. And I see you.

Her eyes filled before mine did, and for a moment we just sat there, staring at each other across the weight of unspoken years. The room was quiet except for our breathing and the hum of the refrigerator in the background, but it felt like time slowed. When she finally leaned into me, I wrapped my arms around her, and it was as though both of us exhaled at the same time. My apology didn't erase the past, but it opened a door. She rested her head on my shoulder, and in that silence, I knew she heard me.

That moment replayed in my mind for days. I kept hearing my own voice, shaky but firm, admitting where I went wrong and telling her I was sorry. For so long, I thought being a good mother meant holding it all together, pretending I never made mistakes. But apologizing to her showed me something different: that being honest about my failures didn't make me weak; it made me trustworthy. She didn't need me to be perfect; she needed me to be present. And in her silence that night, head resting against my shoulder, I realized she wasn't just forgiving me, she was teaching me what grace really looked like.

That changed everything.

Her shoulders softened, her eyes welled with tears, and for the first time in a long time, she leaned into me without hesitation. It wasn't just my words; it was her finally believing them.

We started rebuilding our bond, not through perfection, but through honesty.

Rebuilding looked like late-night talks on her bed, where she asked questions, and I answered without hiding. It looked like Sunday mornings, making pancakes together, the kitchen messy with flour but filled with laughter. It looked like car rides where the music was loud, and the conversation flowed freely, no fear of judgement. These small rituals stitched us back together, thread by thread. What once felt fragile slowly became strong, not because it was flawless, but because it was real.

She knew I was healing. And in that process, she started to heal, too. Eventually, I started thinking about love in relationships again.

It was only after learning to love myself and my daughter differently that I even had the capacity to imagine sharing love again. Healing had to begin at home before it could ever expand outward.

But I knew it had to be different this time.

No more begging to be chosen. No more shrinking to fit someone else's capacity. No more mistaking effort for connection.

This time, love would look like a partnership, mutuality, shared values, and consistency.

I wasn't looking for someone to save me. I had already done that.

Now, I wanted someone who could meet me. At my level. With their peace. With their growth.Because I wasn't building a life from scratch anymore. I was adding to a foundation I had laid with blood, sweat, tears and truth.

Love, for me now, means this:

I can hold myself and still allow someone to hold me.

Now I picture love as quiet mornings when the air feels safe, as conversations that end in understanding rather than shouting, as hands held without fear of letting go. I see it as laughter that comes easily, not forced, and support that doesn't keep score. Love, to me, is no longer about losing myself; it's about building something stronger together, where both people grow without shrinking. That's the kind of love I deserve, and the only kind I'll accept moving forward.

Redefining love wasn't just for me; it was for her, for us, for the legacy we're leaving behind. I want my daughter to grow up knowing love as something steady and kind, not conditional or chaotic. I want her to recognize her worth so deeply that she never confuses struggle with devotion or silence with peace. My story may have started with broken versions of love, but it doesn't have to end there. Love can be rebuilt from ashes, reshaped into something whole, holy, and finally, mine. And that's the story I want carried forward, not of pain endured, but of love redefined.

CHAPTER 18

FROM E1 TO O1E

When I joined the Navy, I was a scared, quiet girl from a broken childhood, with more pain than peace in my pocket. I was an E1-Seaman Recruit, barely knew how to hold a salute, but I knew how to show up.

I can still remember the sting of my first shouted correction at boot camp, my heart racing as I tried to stand taller, to blend in, to not be the one who messed up the line. The uniform felt stiff and foreign against my skin, and the weight of my boots made every step feel heavy, but I wore them like they were my ticket to survival. At night, lying in my rack, the question would creep in louder than the snores of the women around me. The walls felt too close, the lights too dim, and the silence too sharp. I replayed the decision that brought me there, asking myself if I had thrown my life into chaos for nothing. But then I would remind myself that there was no turning back, that the girl I had been was gone, and that the woman I was becoming demanded that I push forward. So I whispered pep talks to myself in the dark, promising that I could survive one more day, one more test, one more whistle.

Each morning when the whistle blew, I pushed those doubts down and laced up my boots again-hungry, determined, tired of running from the ghosts waiting at home.

I didn't walk in with confidence. I built it from the deck plates up.

I threw myself into everything: learning my job, volunteering, watching, listening.

I did the work nobody else wanted to do, not for recognition, but because I knew effort would take me places shortcuts never could.

I volunteered for everything, command clean-ups, collateral duties, you name it. There were nights when the office was quiet and everyone else had gone home, but I stayed behind, combing through instructions, figuring out systems nobody had taken the time to explain. I was determined to know my rate inside and out, because knowledge was something no one could take from me. Those long hours weren't glamorous, but they built a foundation of respect. People noticed, even when they didn't say it out loud.

I earned my pins–surface and air. I deployed twice with the *USS Abraham Lincoln*. I was named Blue Jacket of the Year. When they called my name, the room erupted with claps, and I felt heat rush to my face. I smiled, posed for the photo, shook hands, but inside I was battling the voice that whispered I didn't deserve it. Still, I tucked that award into my binder like it was gold. My shipmates patted me on the back, chiefs and officers nodded their approval, and for a brief moment, I let myself believe that maybe, just maybe, I was good at this Navy thing.

What they didn't see was the war happening inside me. Outwardly, I smiled, accepted their praise, and kept moving as if confidence came naturally. Inwardly, I argued with every compliment, convinced that one day someone would find out I wasn't as capable as they thought. It was like living in two skins at once, the one polished for show, and the one raw and aching underneath. That tug-of-war between recognition and doubt became the rhythm of my career for years.

I left that command with two Navy Achievement medals, dual-qual, E5…and scars I didn't discuss.

But behind the awards and smiles, something darker was forming.

Because while I was being praised on paper, I was also being broken behind closed doors.

Sexual assault. Twice. Words that still feel heavy even now.

And yet I told no one. I walked the passageways with a straight face, saluting officers, answering "aye aye" as if nothing happened. I laughed at jokes in the mess decks, stood tall in inspections, all while my insides screamed. My coping strategy became busyness. If I kept my hands moving, my mind wouldn't wander to the memory I wanted buried. I threw myself into work, took every watch I could, and volunteered for every collateral duty. The more my plate overflowed, the less space I had to feel. But even then, there were nights when the silence was too loud, when the memories clawed their way back no matter how tired I was. What I wanted most back then was for someone to look me in the eyes and say, "You don't have to be okay to be worthy," but no one did, so I told myself and kept marching. The hardest part wasn't just the assault, it was the silence afterward, the way I swallowed my pain because I didn't trust the system to protect me. So I carried it alone, folded neatly behind my ribbons and my smile.

I walked the passageways with a smile, but inside I was fractured, piecing myself together one duty day at a time.

But I didn't let it end me.

I became a SAPR Advocate because no one should ever feel as silenced and confused as I did. My next command was CPRW-11-toxic leadership, but I rose anyway. Pregnant. Still leading. Still showing up. Still setting the standard. There were mornings when my uniform felt tighter by the week, my body aching in ways I couldn't explain, but I still marched onto the quarterdeck ready to lead. I chaired MWR events with swollen ankles, organized fundraisers with heartburn crawling up my throat, and stood in front of Sailors with a smile even when I wanted nothing more than to lie down. Some Sailors looked at me with awe, telling me later that they couldn't believe how much I carried while carrying a child. Others whispered, questioning whether I was cut out for leadership while "distracted" by pregnancy. I heard it all, but I refused to let it stop me. I wanted my Sailors to see that leadership didn't pause for personal milestones, it evolved with them. If anything, being pregnant while leading made me sharper, more determined to prove that compassion and resilience weren't weaknesses but strengths. My pregnancy didn't exempt me; it pushed me. I wanted my daughter to know, even before she arrived, that her mother showed up no matter what.

I was MWR Vice President and Junior Sailor of the Year. I left that command with a 5.0 eval and a vision that was finally getting clearer. Somewhere out of that command, my AO told me, "You're going to make a great officer one day." I laughed, but he wasn't joking. And deep down… Maybe I didn't want him to be.

Then came *the* command-the one where everything shifted—the one where I went from E5 to O1E in one single tour. From the outside, it looked like success. Inside, I was still doubting myself.

I went through a divorce while moving from E5 to E6. I was separated from my daughter, trying to balance rank with reality and losing my footing most days. I could hear her crying over the phone, and that sound never left me. Her little voice on the other end of the line cracked my heart open every time. "When are you coming home, Mommy?" she would ask, and I would swallow hard, trying to steady my voice as I answered. Sometimes I would hang up and sit in silence, staring at the phone log after the call ended, letting the tears fall only when I knew no one could see. I'd sit there trying to stitch myself back together before stepping out to face my Sailors again, forcing my uniform to look sharper than I felt inside. It was the kind of ache that had no remedy, missing milestones, birthdays, bedtime stories. Her voice lingered in my mind long after the call, an echo that reminded me of everything I was working for and everything I was losing at the same time. Those were the sacrifices no ribbon or award could ever balance out-the burden that fueled me and broke me all at once.

Even now, that echo lives in me. It was the sound of my own childhood pain reverberating through her, and the guilt of knowing I couldn't be in two places at once nearly broke me.

I carried that guilt like a weight sewn into my uniform. But I kept pushing. Even through the exhaustion, I never stopped showing up.

I was ecstatic when I picked up E6, finally reaching my goal. After my second year as an E6, I was selected for Sailor of the Year. Chief's exam came around, and I remember my CO stopping me in the p-way and asking me, "How do you think you did on the exam? I shrugged and said, "I don't know, I didn't study. The look on his face said it all – disappointment mixed with surprise. But I was honest. I didn't need to study because I was heavily into my manuals!

I laughed softly, thinking of how far I'd come.

The irony wasn't lost on me. Others burned midnight oil, highlighting pages, swapping flashcards, and drilling each other with questions. I, on the other hand, lived in my manuals, not out of obligation but because I had built my confidence there when everything else felt shaky. What some thought was arrogance was actually survival. I studied that way because I had to believe in something solid. And in that moment, my honesty set me apart. I wasn't just prepared for the exam; I was prepared for the weight of the anchors themselves. Plus, I had too much going on. Too many hats to wear. Still, when I made the board, I was even shocked.

I was even more shocked when I was selected as Chief. I was mad. I won't lie.

It wasn't what I wanted. It wasn't even what I was aiming for. But I made the best of it. Because that's what I do. I rise – even in places I didn't ask to be planted.

While I was an E6, I was at a crossroads – unsure if I wanted to continue toward Chief or pursue a commission as an officer. I sat on a career development board with my CMC and mentor, weighing my options. I was unsure. Scared. Shrinking in the middle of my excellence. I'll never forget what my CMC said to me. Why do you doubt yourself so much? You don't have to fight yourself. We see you. And I broke down.

Because she was right, I had spent my whole life doubting myself. Fighting to be seen. To be worthy. To be enough. And here I was still doing it – even after everything I had accomplished.

I cried in that CDB. I tried to hold it in at first, tried to keep my answers sharp and professional, but when the CMC asked what was really going on, the dam broke. Tears spilled before I could stop them. My hands shook as I spoke about the pressure, the weight of being everything to everyone, the constant fear of not measuring up. And instead of ridicule, I found understanding, heads nodded around the table, and for once, I didn't feel weak for crying; I felt seen.

Tears in uniform felt almost like rebellion. We're trained to stand tall, to keep composure, to swallow our pain. But in that Career Development Board, surrounded by leaders who didn't look away when I broke, I felt a new kind of strength. It wasn't about toughness; it was about trust. Letting them see me cry was my way of admitting that leadership wasn't about being unbreakable. It was about showing up human, even when the weight felt unbearable.

Not because I was weak – but because I was finally letting go of the need to earn love I had already gained.

I applied for LDO the same year I was up for Chief. It felt like I was standing in two worlds – one foot in tradition, the other in transformation.

And somehow, I was selected for both; Chief was first. After I was pinned two months later, the LDO results came out, and I was in a good mood that day. I didn't know the results were out, but I was in a great mood. Then I heard my name over the 1MC to report to the CO's Cabin, and I was like, hmm, I wonder what I did now lol. I walked up the ladder slowly. Once I got near my CO's office, I peered in and saw my complete triad: my CO, XO, and CMC. My CO waved me in. I walk in, and he is like What did you do now? I'm like, I have no idea what I did? And my XO was like Your wardroom dues are due and it took a second to register, but I had been selected for LDO, and I was like This is why I was in such a good mood! They all congratulated me, and as I was walking back to my office in disbelief, my CO came over the 1MC to let everyone know I had been selected for LDO. So many congratulations, so many handshakes, best news of the day.

First time up! For both!

The same people who told me I wouldn't pick up Chief the first time. I did.

The same ones who said I wouldn't pick up LDO the first time?
I did.
I proved them wrong–with grace.
There was a time when my Prior CO and CMC joked about my future
"Will she be a CMC or command a warship?
The answer is:
Whatever I want.

From the outside, they see the uniform, the pins, the pay grade. They don't see the cost of what it took to get here, what I carried through every advancement board, every eval, every duty day. I didn't just earn the rank. I reclaimed my power.

From unseen to unstoppable. From survival to leadership. From E1 to O1E.

This wasn't just a promotion. It was my rebirth.

The girl who once struggled to hold a salute now stood commissioned. And in that moment, I realized I hadn't just risen through the ranks, I had risen through myself.

It felt like being reborn in my own skin. From the deck plates of an E1, scrubbing and standing watch, to standing tall as a chief and an Officer, my journey was more than promotions. It was survival-learned, turned into leadership; silence, turned into voice; pain, turned into purpose. When I pinned on those anchors and bars, I wasn't just celebrating a career milestone. I was saluting the girl who started with nothing and the woman who refused to stay there.

Every stripe, every anchor, every bar was more than a personal achievement; it was a promise. A promise to my daughter that she would inherit a mother who didn't quit. A promise to my Sailors that their struggles could be steppingstones, not stumbling blocks. And a promise to the girl who once lay in her bootcamp rack whispering pep talks in the dark, that she would one day look back and realize she became everything she once doubted she could be.

From the black sheep to O1E, I didn't just rise through the ranks; I rose through myself.

CHAPTER 19

REDEFINING MOTHERHOOD
WHILE IN UNIFORM

Motherhood doesn't pause for rank, and the military doesn't pause for motherhood. Somehow, I learned to keep breathing in both worlds. I had to learn how to hold both–even when both were breaking me.

There were deployments, duty days, schools, and exercises. There were days when I couldn't be there for the first day of school, the field trip, or the bedtime story. There were nights when I heard my daughter cry through the phone. Her voice would crack through the static, and I'd press the phone tighter to my ear, wishing I could climb through the line to hold her. When I hung up, the silence in my room could swallow me whole. Those nights stretched endlessly, the hum of the ship, the flicker of fluorescent lights, even the sound of boots echoing down the passageway felt louder against the silence in my rack. I would stare at the bulkhead, clutching the phone as it could somehow still connect me to her. Sleep never came easily after those calls. On those nights, I built quiet rituals to survive the ache. I would journal until my hand cramped, filling page after page with words I couldn't say out loud. I whispered prayers into the dark, asking God to hold her close when I couldn't. Sometimes I would close my eyes and replay her voice in my head over and over, clinging to

103

the memory of her laughter, the way she said "Mommy" like it carried the whole world inside it. Those rituals didn't erase the distance, but they gave me a thread to hold on to when the separation threatened to pull me apart.

I had to choke back tears to tell her, *Mommy's coming home soon.* I missed milestones I'll never get back. I missed her very first recital. While I was deployed, her dad made sure she was ready, her hair slicked back, her costume pressed, her shoes polished. She stood on stage, tiny and brave, moving to the music with all the energy she had. Later, I saw the pictures: her little arms stretched wide; her smile bright, but her eyes scanning the crowd. She told me afterward that she had looked for me and that she had hoped I would be there. Hearing that shattered something inside me, because I knew that no photo or video could replace the feeling of her seeing my face in the audience.

I told myself she was surrounded by love, that her dad made sure she was dressed perfectly, hair neat, shoes tied, ready for her big moment. And I knew she smiled on stage, but in the quiet after my shift, the guilt sank deep. I wanted her to look out into the crowd and see me clapping until my hands stung. I wanted her to feel the warmth of my presence, not just the sound of my voice replaying on a voicemail later. That guilt followed me like a shadow, reminding me that some sacrifices leave scars on both mother and child.

I also missed her fifth birthday. At that age, Jojo Siwa was her world, bows, glitter, and all things bright and loud. Her dad threw her a JoJo Siwa-themed party, and from the pictures, I could see the balloons, the cake covered in sprinkles, and her wide grin as she posed with her gifts. Everyone made sure she was celebrated, but I wasn't there to light the candles or sing "Happy Birthday." She told me about it over the phone later, her voice filled with excitement, but beneath it I could hear something else, the quiet reality that her mother missed another moment she would never get back. Those milestones haunted me, not because she lacked love, but because I couldn't be the one to give it in those moments. Yet in every photo, I saw proof that she was still thriving, that even when I wasn't there physically, my love still reached her through the life I was building.

When the pictures arrived, I stared at them until they blurred. She was beaming in a glitter bow almost bigger than her head, surrounded by balloons and laughter. I studied every frame trying to imagine the sound of her giggle, the excitement in her voice when she tore open presents. My heart swelled with pride that she was celebrated, but it cracked all the same because my arms weren't the ones hugging her that day. Sometimes the loneliest part of motherhood in uniform wasn't the deployments, it was watching memories happen in pictures instead of in person.

The guilt of that used to eat me alive. But I also showed her something else.

I showed her what strength looks like. I showed her that women can wear uniforms and still love deeply. That we can lead Sailors and still show up to braid hair at 2 a.m.

I can still picture the night I stumbled in from duty, uniform rumpled, body aching, only to find her waiting with a brush in hand. "Can you braid it before school tomorrow?" she whispered, fighting sleep. My eyelids were heavy, but I sat her between my knees on the floor and parted her hair with my tired hands. The rhythm of braiding grounded me, each twist a reminder of why I kept pushing. By the time I tied off the last braid, she had dozed off against my leg, and I carried her to bed with a quiet pride that no rank could match.

I can still smell the faint mix of shampoo and coconut oil as I braided her hair. She leaned against my leg, trusting me with her whole weight, and for those few minutes, the exhaustion of the Navy disappeared. Her small body was warm, steady, and safe, and with every parting and twist, I reminded myself why I sacrificed so much. It wasn't just hair; it was a connection. It was proof that no matter how far I traveled or how long I was gone, these simple, sacred moments stitched us back together.

There were times I questioned if I was doing enough, if I was present enough, if I had damaged her by not always being there physically. But then she started to say things like *I'm proud of you, Mommy,* and *You're the strongest person I know.* And I realized maybe I was doing more right than I gave myself credit for.

Being a mother in uniform meant I sometimes had to parent from afar. It meant relying on FaceTime when I wanted to hold her hand. It meant apologizing often. But it also meant showing her what resilience looks like in real time.

There were hard conversations. "Why do you always have to leave?" she asked me once, her voice sharp with the kind of honesty only a child can give. My throat tightened. "Because this is my job, baby. Because I'm serving so you can have a better life." She crossed her arms, frowning. "But I just want you here." And in that moment, no uniform, no award, no speech could make up for the truth in her eyes. I sat with her, letting the silence hold us both, wishing I could give her the life she deserved without her ever having to walk away. That night, I realized love sometimes means breaking your own heart to build a better world for your child.

I held it together in front of her, nodding, validating her pain, swallowing my own tears so she could see my strength. But later, when I was alone, I let it all out. I wept into my hands, the sobs shaking through me, because her honesty pierced me deeper than any criticism from a superior ever could. Her eyes reminded me that my daughter didn't need a decorated officer; she needed her mother. And in that truth was harder to face than any uniform inspection I'd ever endured.

Moments when she didn't understand why I had to leave again. Why couldn't I always protect her from what was happening at home?

I made her a promise. *No matter where I am, you matter most.* I whispered that promise into her hair as I tucked her in, pressing my lips against her forehead. She didn't say anything right away, but she held onto my shirt like she was anchoring herself to my words. From that night forward, I carried her with me into every space, every brief, into inspections, onto ships. If I was there, she was too, in spirit. That vow became my compass. Anytime I questioned if I was enough, I went back to that moment, to the way her small hand clutched me like I was her whole world.

I started involving her in my growth, letting her see the books I read, telling her what rank I was working toward, and explaining what courage meant. Motherhood wasn't just something I did; it became a reason for how hard I fought to become more.

Because every time I advanced, I thought of her.

Every board I sat in front of.

Every eval I turned in.

Every time I chose to keep going.

I wanted her to see that nothing about our life disqualified us from building a better one.

I may not have always been there every moment, but I was present in every way that mattered.

And now?

She's becoming her version of strong—not because I was perfect…but because I kept showing up.

At my commissioning ceremony, she placed my cover on my head. Her hands trembled slightly, and I could see her lip caught between her teeth. In that small hesitation, I realized she carried the weight of all the years I had missed, and yet, in that kiss, she gave me forgiveness I hadn't even asked for. The room held its breath as she stood on her tiptoes, stretching to reach me. Cameras clicked, people smiled, but in my mind, it was just the two of us. I felt the weight of the cover not just as a symbol of rank, but as a crown she placed on my head with forgiveness and pride. My heart pounded, and I fought back tears as I looked into her eyes. They weren't just proud, they were steady, like she finally believed that all my sacrifices had meaning. In that instant, every missed bedtime, every tearful phone call, every doubt was folded into this moment of recognition between us.

For a moment, the crowd faded away. The sound of cameras clicking, chairs creaking, even the applause, all of it disappeared. All I could see was her. The pride in her eyes wasn't polished or rehearsed; it was raw, a reflection of everything we had survived together. When she placed that cover on my head, I didn't just feel like an officer; I felt like a mother redeemed. That ceremony wasn't about rank anymore; it was about reconciliation, about her finally seeing the meaning behind all the nights apart, the birthdays missed, the sacrifices that had nearly broken us.

When she leaned down and kissed me, I saw it in her eyes-admiration, pride, awe.

Her mom—her provider, protector, and role model rose above it all.

And in that moment, I knew motherhood and uniform had never been separate. They were both battlegrounds, where I learned how to fight, how to love, and how to endure. Together, they made me who I am.

Redefining motherhood while in uniform was never about choosing one role over the other - it was about weaving them together into something unshakeable. My daughter has seen me in every state: strong, broken, determined, exhausted, triumphant. And through it all, she has learned that love is not erased by distance, and strength is not ruined by imperfection. The legacy I hope to leave her is simple: that she can chase her calling without apology and still love fiercely. My story is proof that it's possible, and my prayer is that hers be written with fewer scars and even greater joy.

That moment will stay with me forever.

Chapter 20

The Weight of the Uniform

Making rank is one thing. Carrying it is another.

People think the fight gets easier once you put on the anchors or are commissioned as an officer. But the truth is–the fight changes. It goes from proving yourself to holding yourself together.

Every morning, as I buttoned my khakis and placed my cover on my head, I felt a shift in my body. The fabric itself wasn't heavy, but the meaning stitched into it weighed me down. The anchors on my collar gleamed, sharp enough to cut, and I often wondered if they were cutting into me as much as they were shining for others to see. Adjusting my gig line in the mirror wasn't just about appearance; it was about preparing for battle, not against enemies overseas, but against the quiet wars waged in conference rooms and mess decks.

Every morning before stepping out, I didn't just put on my uniform; I braced myself for battle. I reminded myself that I might be tested in ways that had nothing to do with my job; questioned in meetings, under-estimated in briefings, dismissed before I even spoke. That was the true weight of the uniform, knowing I had to be excellent before I even opened my mouth. By the time I walked out the door, my face looked composed.

The uniform got heavier at the top. Not just the fabric, but expectations stitched into it. The eyes. The whispers. The way presence alone makes others uncomfortable–especially when you're the only one who looks like you in the room.

For some time, I was the only female and the only black woman in my first-class mess. Walking into that space wasn't about grabbing food; it was about stepping into a room where reputations were built, and respect was tested. The air carried a charge, a mix of authority and competition, and every eye seemed to measure me as I entered. Laughter and conversations often dipped for a split second, just long enough for me to notice before they picked back up. I sat through meetings with my back straight, speaking only when I knew my words couldn't be dismissed, careful to balance firmness with diplomacy. It was a constant reminder that I wasn't just representing myself, I was representing every woman and every Black Sailor who might come after me. The first-class mess was supposed to be a place of camaraderie, but often it felt like sitting in a room where the joke ended just before I walked in. Laughter hushed, conversations shifted, eyes darted. I learned quickly to read the temperature of the room before speaking, who leaned in, who leaned back, who was ready to dismiss me before I even finished my thought. Some days, the silence was louder than any insult. It was a peculiar kind of isolation, being so visible I could never disappear, and yet so invisible I often wondered if my voice registered at all. The expectations doubled, tripled, even. Sharp, but not too sharp. Firm, but not too firm. Visible, but not too visible. Any misstep would be remembered, magnified, and repeated. The margin for error was razor-thin, and I knew I had to live inside it every day.

Vice president. Eyes rolled when I spoke. Suggestions were dismissed until someone else said the same thing louder. I led anyway.

When I picked up Chief, it was more of the same. Suddenly, I wasn't just a Sailor–I was a symbol. I had to be sharp, but not too sharp. Firm, but not aggressive. Smart, but never threatening. One wrong move was *"That's why we don't promote people like her."*

The double standard was absolute. I was expected to do more, carry more, smile more, just to be seen as an equal. There were days I wanted to scream. I wanted to take off the khakis, the anchors, the pressure, and breathe.

But I didn't.

Because I knew what it meant for someone like me to be standing in that space. I knew what it meant for the junior Sailor watching from the back of the room, whispering to herself, *If she can do it, I can too.*

It wasn't just about me, though. My presence became a mirror for others. I'll never forget when one of my junior sailors pulled me aside, nervous but determined. Her voice shook as she said, "Ma'am, I just wanted to say thank you. Seeing you up there makes me feel like I can make it too. That moment hit deeper than any award ever could. It reminded me that my survival was about more than me. It was proof. Proof that the next generation could push through, that the path, though heavy, was still walkable. Her words followed me long after she left my office. On nights when exhaustion sank deep into my bones, I replayed them in my mind like a song. "You made me believe I could stay." That sentence became my anchor. It reminded me that my presence had power, that simply existing and surviving in these spaces was enough to give someone else courage. I began to understand that my story wasn't just mine; it was a lantern. My Sailors didn't need me to be perfect; they needed me to be proof that survival was possible, even in the heaviest seasons.

So, I carried the weight, not just for me, but for everyone who had been silenced, overlooked, passed over, or told to wait their turn.

I remember one day I was speaking passionately about something that mattered deeply to me—something I knew could make things better for the command. I was animated, energized, and determined. It wasn't just about carrying rank; it was about surviving perception. During Chief season, I learned quickly that even spaces meant for mentorship could carry bias. One day, in the middle of a session designed to shape me into the leader I was becoming, someone looked at me and said, "Why are you so angry?" It wasn't asked with concern; it was launched like an accusation. My stomach clenched, but I kept my face neutral. Inside, I wanted to say that my tone was conviction, not aggression. But as a black woman,

I knew those explanations rarely mattered. So I swallowed the sting, held my posture, and let that moment sharpen me instead of silence me.

Inside, though, the conflict was sharp. Part of me wanted to defend myself, to explain that being direct wasn't the same as being angry, that holding people accountable wasn't aggression, it was leadership. But another part of me knew the truth: my words would be dissected, my tone judged, my intent twisted. I stood there rehearsing the arguments in my head, silently debating what I could say without giving them more ammunition. That's the exhausting part most people never see, the mental gymnastics of editing yourself in real time, to avoid being reduced to a stereotype.

Inside, I wanted to shout: *Do you not see the passion? The dedication? Why must my fire always be read as fury?* But I swallowed it, because in that space, my silence was my survival.

I blinked. "I'm not angry, I said. "Just passionate about what I do." But then, I realized that my passion was read as aggression. My tone was policed. My intensity labeled

Another time, I was about to be debriefed by my CO while standing with my department head. I reached into my pocket and applied some lip balm–nothing major, just me keeping myself together. He looked over at me and spoke. "What are you doing that for? Your eval is already signed?"

I stood there stunned.

Like me, moisturizing my lips somehow meant I was trying to seduce someone, as if my professionalism, rank, and position disappeared when I did something as simple as apply Chapstick. He made it sound like I was glossing them to go in and sexually perform for my CO.

It was disgusting. And it wasn't very comfortable.

It didn't happen in some casual hallway exchange; it happened right before I was about to be debriefed by my Commanding Officer. The gravity of the moment was already enough to make my pulse quicken. And then, suddenly, someone decided my lip balm was worth turning into a spectacle. My cheeks burned, not with shame, but with the audacity of being reduced to something so trivial when everything else I carried was monumental. I held my composure, walked into that debrief with my head high, and handled my business. But later, when I replayed it, I realized how intentional those little cuts could be. They were meant to distract, to shrink me, to remind me that no matter how perfect my uniform looked, there would always be someone trying to strip it down. That's when I made a decision, dignity would always be my answer.

Something so small as lip balm revealed so much. The sting wasn't just in the words; it was in the way they were delivered, casual, dismissive, meant to shrink me into something less than I was. I remember sitting in that office afterward, gripping my notebook, reminding myself not to cry, not to give them the satisfaction. I told myself in that moment that I would never let anyone make me feel less than what I had earned. If they wanted to reduce me, I would rise higher. If they wanted me to shrink, I would stand taller. Dignity became my quiet rebellion.

My stomach turned, heat rising in my face as I forced a steady expression. I learned then that sometimes professionalism meant carrying shame that wasn't even mine.

That moment wasn't just inappropriate, it was a reminder of how easily women in uniform are sexualized for existing. How quickly we're stripped of dignity with a single comment, like our presence, our femininity is always up for debate or interpretation.

But I held my head high. Because I knew who he was, and I wasn't going to let his small-mindedness shrink my excellence

And still, I didn't shrink.

There is power in presence, even when they act like you don't belong, even when they try to shrink you, even when they want you quiet. Your existence disrupts their comfort. And that is precisely why you were called to be there.

The weight of the uniform never broke me, because it was never just about the rank on my chest–it was about the character underneath it.

I earned every chevron, every pin, the bar, and every salute. Not through perfection but through resilience.

Because carrying the weight of the uniform was never about fabric or metal. It was about proving, every day, that my presence had a purpose, even when the room wanted me gone. Wearing that uniform has never been just about rank or pay grade; it has been about legacy. I carry the weight not only for the girl who started at E1 with trembling hands but for every woman, every Sailor of color, every person who has ever wondered if they belonged in spaces not built for them.

My shoulders ache sometimes under the load, but I remind myself that this weight is also a crown. And if bearing it means the next generation gets to walk a little freer, then I will carry it with pride until the day I hang it up.

Because the weight of the uniform is more than the fabric and rank, it's an inheritance. I carry the weight of those who came before me, the ones who fought battles I'll never know, so that I could stand where I am today. And I carry the weight for those who will come after me, so they might walk into rooms where their voices aren't questioned, where their presence isn't debated, where they don't have to armor themselves every morning just to be seen.

The weight is heavy, yes. But it is also a crown. And until the day I hang it up, I'll wear it proudly, knowing every step I take lightens the load for the next woman who dares to put it on.

CHAPTER 21

LEADING WITHOUT PERMISSION

At some point, I stopped waiting to be accepted. I stopped shrinking. Stopped apologizing. Stopped asking if my presence was too much. Because I had spent years trying to lead the right way, their way.

I can still see myself in those early meetings, sitting in the mess with my ideas burning a hole in my chest, but my mouth shut tight. I would watch others dominate the conversation, throwing out half-formed suggestions while I sat on fully thought-out solutions. I was so afraid of being labeled "too much" that I made myself smaller on purpose. I remember gripping my pen until my fingers hurt, scribbling down notes that should have been spoken out loud. When I walked out of those rooms, my silence echoed louder than anything I could have said, and it ate away at me. That was the kind of shrinking I had to unlearn.

The silence didn't just stay in the room; it stayed in my body. I carried it in my chest, a weight that made breathing tight and shallow. At night, I'd replay the missed moments in my rack, mouthing the words I should have said, knowing it was too late. Headaches came more often, born from holding back thoughts that needed release. It wasn't just about speaking; it was about claiming space. And each time I swallowed my words, a little piece of me wondered if I had lost the chance to prove I belonged.

Their way looked like swallowing my ideas in the mess, nodding when I wanted to push back, forcing myself smaller so I wouldn't be labeled "too much." It was leadership by erasure, and it nearly erased me. Measured. Controlled. And it almost broke me.

So, I changed the rules.

I led from the gut. I led with the heart.

One night, one of my Sailors came to me, overwhelmed. They were struggling with their partner, and the weight of it was written all over their face. They were scheduled for the 2200 to 0200 watch, but admitted quietly that they didn't think they could make it through. Instead of brushing it off or threatening consequences, I told them to take care of themselves, and I would cover their watch. Standing there in the stillness of the night, the red lights glowing dimly, I thought about how leadership isn't just about orders. Sometimes it's about knowing when your people are carrying more than they can bear. That sailor never forgot that moment, and neither did I. That's when I realized leadership wasn't about being perfect; it was about being present.

Later, that same Sailor came to me with a quiet gratitude in their eyes. They didn't need to say much-I could see it in the way they carried themselves differently after that night, a little lighter, a little steadier. Trust had been built in that exchange, not from a briefing or a speech, but from presence. What humbled me most wasn't the recognition; it was realizing how my authenticity gave others permission to be themselves. From that point on, I noticed them watching how I led, leaning in a little closer when I spoke, giving me their best effort without me ever having to ask. One watch turned into a bond, a reminder that leadership is earned in the smallest, most human moments.

I showed up as my whole self, not the sanitized version they were more comfortable with.

And guess what? We still got results.

Because I knew what it felt like to show up, give your all, and still feel unseen. We still accomplished the mission. And my people followed me because they felt seen, not silenced.

I didn't lead through fear. I led through presence. I listened. I advocated. I corrected when needed, but I didn't humiliate.

One of the best decisions I made was cross-training my Sailors. I didn't want them stuck in their lanes, only knowing one side of the work. I wanted them to see the full picture, so that when manning dropped, and it always did, no one would be left scrambling. At first, they groaned about it. Why should they learn jobs that weren't theirs? But I stood firm, telling them, "You may not always like it now, but one day you'll thank me." That day came faster than they expected. When our section went short, my team stepped in without missing a beat. Watching them switch roles seamlessly, confident and capable, I knew the effort had been worth it. That was leadership, too, raising the bar without tearing anyone down.

As I stood back, I felt a swell of pride that no award could capture. Watching them move like a well-oiled machine, stepping into each other's roles with confidence, I knew this was the fruit of every late-night training session, every explanation repeated until it stuck. Even the Chiefs and Officers watching took note, impressed at how fluidly the team operated. That day proved that my vision of cross-training wasn't just an idea, it was a force multiplier, a living example of leadership rippling outward.

Because I knew what it felt like to be under leadership that made you feel like you didn't matter. And I refused to recreate that pain for anyone else.

Leadership is not about barking orders. It's about building people. It's about standing in the fire with them, not above them. It's about knowing who you are, so you don't get lost in the uniform.

I used to think I had to lead like a man to be respected. I thought compassion was a weakness. That softness had no place in command.

But I learned the truth: You can be soft and firm. You can correct it with kindness. You can protect your people while protecting your peace.

I stopped trying to sound like them. I stopped trying to win them over. I stopped waiting for permission. I started building the kind of leadership I wish I had.

And the more I leaned into my truth, the more powerful I became.

What humbled me most wasn't the rank, it was the impact.

I constantly mentored sailors, some of whom did not even realize it. I was just being myself, showing up fully, and doing the work. One day, after picking up Chief and being picked up for LDO, I was walking through the hangar bay, and one of the junior Sailors looked at me and said, "You are the GOAT."

The words caught me off guard in the middle of the hangar bay. The air carried the sharp tang of saltwater mixed with oil, and the metal deck echoed with every boot step. A helicopter sat quietly in the corner, blades tied down, the space unusually still compared to the bustle of flight quarters. It wasn't the kind of place you expected a compliment; it was a space for work, sweat, and steel nerves. Yet in that moment, a young Sailor looked at me with a grin and said, "You are the GOAT." They almost laughed as the words slipped out, like they hadn't meant to say it out loud, then quickly nodded and busied themselves again. I laughed too, brushing it off, but later those words stayed with me. Greatest of all time. It wasn't about ego; it was about impact. In that loud, gritty ship's hangar, surrounded by salt and steel, I realized my leadership wasn't just seen, it was felt.

For so much of my career, I had poured into others without expecting recognition. That's what leaders do-we give and give, often without hearing how much it mattered. So when the words, "You're the GOAT," reached me, it landed heavier than they knew. It was rare for someone to say it out loud, rarer still for it to come from a peer. It reminded me that impact isn't always visible, but it is always felt. And in that moment, I allowed myself to take it in, to accept that I wasn't just working hard-I was making a difference.

I froze midstep. The hangar bay was loud with chatter and metal echoing under boots, but in that moment. All I could hear was his voice. His grin was wide, his eyes bright, like he had been waiting for the chance to tell me. That single sentence carried the weight of every unseen battle I had fought.

That moment hit me hard–because my entire career had almost been ruined just a year before. By people I could trust. Betrayal cuts the deepest when it comes from inside the ranks. The year before, my career dangled on the edge of collapse because of whispers and accusations. People I had worked beside looked at me differently, like I was guilty of something they couldn't even name. I walked around with a weight in my chest, knowing one wrong move could be twisted against me. Nights were long, sleep was short, my mind running circles around what I could lose.

But I didn't fold. I showed up every day, sharper, more precise, more unshakeable. Every watch stood, every Sailor developed, every inspection passed became my rebuttal. I refused to let rumors decide my future. Slowly, the same people who doubted me couldn't ignore the evidence: I wasn't going anywhere.

That year, paranoia became a constant companion. I found myself double-checking every email before hitting send, rehearsing every sentence before speaking in meetings, scanning my face in the mirror to make sure my expression couldn't be misread. The stress settled in my shoulders, a constant ache, and in my stomach, a knot that never fully loosened. Yet even under the microscope, I refused to let them break me. If anything, it sharpened me. I learned how to be deliberate with my words, intentional with my moves, and unshakable in my presence. They could watch all they wanted-what they saw was resilience.

People who were threatened by my presence.

But I didn't let it stop me.

I kept showing up. I kept leading.

And they watched me rise.

I wasn't just leading a team. I was leading a movement, a quiet, unshakeable reminder that you don't have to become someone else to lead effectively. You have to become yourself fully.

Because the truth was simple: I stopped waiting for permission. I started leading. Leading without permission became my legacy. I stopped waiting for validation and started becoming the example I once wished I had. My daughter, my Sailors, and those still finding their voices needed to see that leadership doesn't always look like the manual says it should. Sometimes it looks like standing a midnight watch for someone who can't or training your people so they can carry the mission no matter what. Sometimes it looks like love disguised as discipline-if that makes me different, then I'll wear it proudly. I'd rather leave behind a career lit with authenticity than one polished by silence.

Because the truth is, I'm not just writing my story-I'm leaving a map. A map for my daughter, for my Sailors, and for every woman who has ever swallowed her truth to survive.

CHAPTER 22

—⟋⟍—

CHOOSING MYSELF, AGAIN AND AGAIN

There comes a point where surviving isn't enough anymore. Checking boxes, making ranks, and keeping the peace can't cover what's breaking inside you. I reached that point.

I had to stop pretending I was okay. I had to stop letting other people's comfort come before my truth. Had to stop making space for people who wouldn't make space for me.

That meant walking away from certain relationships, even if they were familiar, even if they had history. Even if part of me still wanted to make it work. Because no matter how much I loved them, I was losing myself. And I had spent too long fighting to find her.

When I separated from my second partner, I felt peace I didn't even know existed. The first night alone was almost unnerving in its silence. No arguments echoing down the hall, no slamming doors, no forced small talk—just stillness. I remember curling up on the couch with a blanket, the only sound the hum of the fridge in the kitchen. At first, the quiet felt foreign, too empty. But then I realized it was peaceful. I breathed deeper, slower, and for the first time in years, my body wasn't bracing for the next storm. That night, I slept with the lights off and the window cracked open, letting the cool air remind me I was free.

I slept.

When I woke up the next morning, it felt different than any morning before. The air was still, but it wasn't heavy; it was light, like the house itself was finally exhaling with me. I made coffee slowly, without rushing, letting the sound of the brew fill the silence. I opened the blinds wide and let the sun pour in, not worried about whether anyone else approved. Even something as small as walking barefoot across the cool floor reminded me: this was my space, my freedom, my new beginning.

I started enjoying my home again.

I changed it – got rid of things, added things – and with each day, it felt a little more like mine. We had a room that was supposed to be a movie room, but it was left unfinished – just like so much else. The so-called movie room wasn't much, just a couch pushed against the wall and a mounted TV that rarely got used. Every time I walked past it, it reminded me of wasted space and plans that never became real. After the separation, I finally gave myself permission to make it what I had always wanted: a dining room. I took the couch out, rearranged the space, and brought in a table where conversations could happen and meals could be shared. It wasn't just about furniture; it was about creating a home that reflected me, not a placeholder for someone else's broken promises. Every meal at that table felt like a small victory, proof that I could reshape not just a room, but my life.

I remember standing in that dining room after I transformed it, running my hand across the polished table, setting plates that weren't just for eating but for gathering. I added little touches, such as candles, framed photos, and chairs, that made people want to linger. It was more than furniture. It was a declaration that I would no longer live in a space; I would shape it. Every dinner I hosted there, every laugh that bounced off those walls, became a brick in the new foundation I was building for myself and my daughter.

Every dinner I hosted there reminded me that I was learning to show up for myself. That room became proof that I could build beauty out of what was once disappointment.

So, I transformed it into an elegant dining room, a space that finally felt warm, intentional, and mine. A little more peaceful.

One of my friends told me, "I hope you two work it out. He tried hard to please you," and I remember thinking, "Wow." You have no idea. What you saw was the version he wanted you to see.

It was one of the many masks he wore.

When it was just us in the home, he was mean, nasty, and emotionally closed off. But the moment others were around, he'd switch – suddenly warm, suddenly affectionate, the doting partner he wanted everyone to believe he was.

It wasn't just with neighbors. Around family, he could become the perfect son or the charming in-law, cracking jokes and playing the supportive partner. On social media, he knew exactly how to post smiling pictures, painting a picture of us that looked effortless. People would comment things like "couple goals" not realizing I was sitting just out of frame, silent and exhausted from the argument we'd had moments before. That switch was his greatest performance, but also my greatest prison. I was the only one who knew the truth behind the curtain.

The hardest part was how convincing he could be. He wore his mask so well that sometimes I questioned my own reality. Could I be overreacting? Would anyone ever believe me if I told them? Living with someone who could shift personas so easily was exhausting; it kept me on edge, waiting for which version of him would walk through the door. That constant performance wore me down, making me doubt myself even when my instincts screamed the truth.

And if I ever called it out, I became the problem.

I remember one time I was heading to brunch with a girlfriend. I had just gotten my hair blown out, and it started raining. I asked him to grab the umbrella from the car so my hair wouldn't get wet, and he looked at me and said, "If you bring me back something, I'll grab the umbrella." That day I wore pink. It was my friend's birthday, and we were headed to brunch to celebrate her. The sky was cloudy, but I didn't think much of it until the rain started pouring. I laughed at first, holding my wallet close, trying to cover my hair with my hands as the water dripped onto my dress. I looked back at the house, expecting him to come outside with the umbrella like he said he would, but the door never opened. My friend and I just looked at each other and said, "Wow."

In that moment, something inside me snapped into focus. Watching my friend witness his carelessness, I realized I had been normalizing what should never have been acceptable. I had been explaining away his dismissals, brushing off his indifference as stress or distraction. But when someone else saw it plain as day, I couldn't hide it anymore. It was a mirror held up to me, and I didn't like what I saw: how much I had tolerated, how low I had set the bar. That umbrella wasn't just about the weather; it was a mirror.

Her raised eyebrows said it all. I didn't even have to explain. In that small exchange, I realized how absurd it had become to expect the bare minimum.

He would go out of his way to help our neighbor – anything she needed; he was right there. But at home, I had to beg for the most minor things.

He begged and pleaded that things would be different. And I tried – because I wanted to believe him.

But every time, that mask would slip. And I'd see it again – the performance, the manipulation, the empty promises. He was playing a part. Saying what he thought I wanted to hear. But his actions always told the truth.

Choosing myself didn't come easily. It came with guilt. Second-guessing. Lonely nights.

There were nights I stared at the ceiling, replaying conversations in my head, wondering if I was the problem. But deep down, I knew the real problem was shrinking to fit into love that wasn't love at all.

But it also came with peace. Peace in knowing I didn't have to chase love anymore. Peace in knowing I could stand on my own. Peace in finally believing I was enough without proving it to anybody.

The silence in my house pushed me toward reflection. I had a choice: fill it with distractions, or finally sit with myself. For the first time in years, I chose me.

I started pouring into myself. I went to therapy. I prayed. I reflected.

One day in therapy, I admitted out loud for the first time that I had been trying to fix someone who never wanted to be fixed. Saying the words lifted the weight I didn't even know I was carrying. My therapist looked at me and simply said, "And what would it look like if you stopped?" I didn't have an answer right away, but I carried that question with me into prayer. In prayer, I found my answer: it would look like me choosing me. It would look like giving my daughter a mother who wasn't drained and depleted. It would look like freedom. That realization became my turning point.

Freedom wasn't abstract anymore; it was tangible. It looked like laughing without immediately checking the room to see if it was too loud. It looked like sleeping through the night without fear of waking up to tension in the air. It looked like cooking a meal and enjoying it, instead of holding my breath waiting for criticism. Freedom wasn't just leaving him; it was returning to myself. It was giving my daughter a version of me who wasn't surviving but living.

I created space for joy. I stopped ignoring the signs and started honoring what I needed.

People didn't always understand. Some called it selfish, but I call it survival with intention. I had survived so much already; now it was time to thrive.

And that began with choosing myself. Over and over. Without apology.

Because for the first time in a long time, I chose peace over performance, truth over pretending, and me over survival. Leaving wasn't just about ending a relationship; it was about reclaiming myself. Survival had kept me going for years, but peace gave me the space to thrive. Choosing myself wasn't selfish; it was necessary. It was the difference between living in fragments and living whole. I no longer measure my worth by what I endured for someone else. I measure it by the peace I protect, the love I pour into my daughter, and the truth I refuse to compromise. This time, I'm not just surviving, I'm living.

Choosing myself became an act of legacy. I wanted my daughter to see that love isn't supposed to deplete you, that peace isn't negotiable, and that walking away doesn't mean you failed; it means you refused to abandon yourself. I wanted her to grow up with a new blueprint, one that showed strength not just in staying, but in leaving when leaving was the only path to wholeness. It took me years to understand that peace isn't a destination, it's a discipline. And for every woman who has ever stood at that same crossroads, I wanted my story to whisper you are allowed to choose you, again and again.

CHAPTER 23

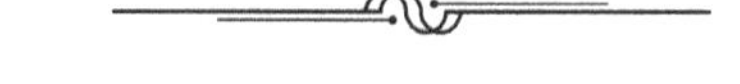

REAWAKENING JOY

After everything I had survived – the trauma, the betrayal, the heartbreak, the silence – joy had to be relearned.

I had poured so much into surviving that I didn't realize I had stopped living.

That changed when I went to Aruba with one of my girlfriends for her birthday. I didn't know how much I needed that trip until I was already there – sun on my skin, laughter in my chest, moving without urgency.

The water in Aruba was the clearest blue I had ever seen, stretching out like glass that caught the light and tossed it back in diamonds. My girlfriend and I spent hours with sand between our toes, sipping drinks that tasted like sugar and citrus, watching the waves chase each other to the shore. At night, we danced until our legs ached, music pounding through the streets, strangers becoming instant friends. Somewhere between the rhythm of the drums and the sound of our laughter, I realized how long it had been since I felt that free. I wasn't looking over my shoulder, I wasn't worrying about who I had to take care of. I was just alive, and it felt foreign and familiar all at once.

What most people didn't see was that Aruba was also the moment I realized how deeply depressed I was. I remember standing on the edge of a cliff, the wind whipping my hair, the ocean stretching out endlessly below. For a split second, I thought about just letting go, falling forward, disappearing into the water, ending the ache I carried. Instead, I masked it. I smiled for a photo, my hair blowing in the wind, and posted it with the caption: "This is what depression looks like." No one noticed the words. They just liked the picture. That smile wasn't for vanity; it was armor. That moment stayed with me, not as shame, but as truth. It was the turning point where I began to understand how easily we hide pain behind curated smiles, and how badly I needed to stop hiding mine. It struck me then how long it had been since I felt that free. Years of responsibility had hardened me, and joy had become something rare, something I rationed rather than fully embracing. But standing there, letting the ocean breeze tangle my hair and the sun warm my shoulders, I remembered the version of myself who once laughed without guilt and dreamed without limits. Aruba didn't just give me rest, it gave me back a piece of the girl I thought I had lost.

I remember dancing barefoot in the sand, music spilling from the beach bar, and realizing I hadn't felt this free in years. It hit me:

I had been depressed.

And this trip – the ease, the laughter, the stillness – reminded me of what freedom felt like.

It wasn't just a vacation. It was a shift.

After that, the joy kept coming.

The following year, I flew to Hawaii for the commissioning ceremony of a good friend I had mentored – someone I had once stood alongside as a ship's secretary on a destroyer.

Watching him rise and be honored for the leader he had become filled me with pride and hope.

I remembered him a year or so before, back when we were both Ship Secretaries on our Destroyers. He was sharp, meticulous, always with a stack of papers in his hand and a smile that never faded, no matter how chaotic the day became. Seeing him now in Hawaii, standing tall in his whites as the crowd cheered, felt like a full-circle moment. The air was warm, fragrant with plumeria, and the sound of waves crashing in the distance blended with the applause. When I placed his cover on his head, my hands trembled for just a second. It wasn't just part of the ceremony;

it was a moment that carried every late night, every sacrifice, every ounce of resilience. In that gesture, I felt the weight of our journey and the pride of knowing we both had risen. His growth, his perseverance, and the reminder that we are not defined by where we start, but by how we keep showing up.

As I stood watching, I felt time fold in on itself, from the chaos of our early careers to this moment of triumph. I couldn't help but think about how many times I had questioned my own path. Standing there as his mentor and his sister in arms, I realized this was proof that the seeds we plant in others can outlive our own doubts. His victory became a mirror, showing me what resilience looks like when it's nurtured, not just endured. It reminded me of the day I earned my own commission, and how it felt to have people believe in me when I couldn't fully believe in myself. Hawaii wasn't just his milestone; it was a reminder that my work mattered, too.

Our friendship flourished from those early ship days, and now we're witnessing each other become.

Then came Miami, a family trip with my daughter and my friends. We started doing annual trips like that, rebuilding family, fun, laughter, and memories. No drama. No fear. Just us.

One afternoon, we sat at the beach, my daughter splashing with my friends' kids, laughter echoing through the air. It was ordinary, simple, and for once, safe. That's what made it extraordinary. Miami was alive with energy, music spilling out of restaurants, the salty breeze rushing in from the ocean, and children's laughter rising above all. I can still see my daughter's hair flying as she ran down the beach, chasing waves and squealing when they caught her ankles. Her cheeks glowed from the sun, and her eyes lit up in a way that told me she felt safe, unburdened. Watching her, I realized how important it was that she saw me smile too. For so long, she had seen me carry heaviness, but here, in this moment, she was watching her mother dance in the sand, laugh with abandon, and breathe without weight on her chest. That was just as much a gift to her as it was to me.

I will never forget the way my daughter looked at me that weekend, watching me laugh, eat good food, and dance like no one was watching.

Her eyes lit up like she was seeing a new side of me, one that wasn't tired or tense but fully alive. I realized in that moment that she was learning just as much from how I healed as she had from how I endured. By showing her that joy could exist after struggle, I was rewriting the story she would carry about what love and womanhood could look like.

And then – Belize.

At the end of that year, I went to Belize, and everything changed.

The streets of Belize buzzed with life, vendors calling out in Spanish and Creole, the smell of grilled meats and spices floating through the air, and children darting between colorful stalls. We pedaled slowly, soaking it all in, our laughter bouncing off cobblestone streets. Later, I found myself face to face with sharks in the water, my heart pounding as I slipped into the sea. Fear gave way to awe as I swam alongside them, their sleek bodies cutting through the water with effortless grace. Belize was different; it was peaceful, almost eerily peaceful, the kind of calm that felt foreign but deeply needed. We spent the days soaking it all in, and one of my favorite memories was riding bikes an hour to the secret beach. The locals looked at us like we were crazy, warning us about how far it was, but we laughed the whole way, pushing through the heat and feeling like kids again when we finally made it. Later, we rode a golf cart through the city, sang karaoke at a little bar, and even managed to get a ticket that we couldn't stop laughing about. But the water, oh, the water is where Belize really gave me back something I didn't know I had lost. When we swam with sharks and stingrays, I was literally laughing and screaming at the same time, splashing around like a child. My friend was fearless, running her hands across the stingray's slick skin, while I clung to the host's back as his co-host tried to place one on me. It was terrifying and hilarious all at once. For those moments, I wasn't a mother, a Sailor, or a woman carrying the weight of survival; I was just Diana, free, playful, and fully alive.

We rode bikes through the city. We swam with sharks and stingrays. We laughed under the stars and ate food that felt like soul on a plate.

And I felt real, embodied, unfiltered joy for the first time in years.

Not the performative kind. Not the "pretend to be okay" kind.

But the kind that wakes you up from the inside.

In Belize, I felt a reawakening. A rebirth. A reminder that I wasn't just healing, I was living again.

And this time, I was doing it for me.

Unapologetically.

Unfiltered

Fully alive.

Joy, I learned, isn't just about the trips or the laughter; it's about reclaiming the parts of yourself you thought were gone forever. It's about building a life that's gone forever. It's about building a life where peace isn't the exception but the standard. From here forward, I vowed to protect that joy fiercely. Not everyone would understand it, and not everyone was meant to share it with me. But it was mine, unapologetic, unfiltered and fully alive, and I refused to let it be stolen again.

Aruba had been the place where I stood on a cliff and silently wondered if life was worth holding on to. The fact that I could go from that moment of despair to later dancing in Miami, celebrating in Hawaii, and laughing in Belize showed me just how far I had come. Joy, for me, was no longer just happiness; it was survival. Choosing to live, to smile, to love again was an act of defiance against everything that tried to break me. And as I held on to that truth, I knew I was passing down something priceless to my daughter: the reminder that even in the deepest valleys, joy is possible and sometimes joy itself is the reason we keep going. And maybe that's what healing really is, remembering how to dance even after you've survived the storm. But even as the waves calmed me, I knew true peace wouldn't come from miles traveled; it had to come from within.

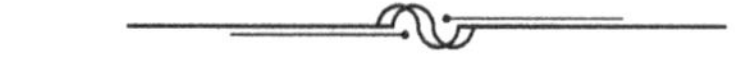

CHAPTER 24

LEGACY IN MOTION

When I was younger in my career, I thought legacy meant having your name etched on a building, a portrait hanging on a wall, or being the kind of leader remembered in speeches decades later. Walking through the command buildings, I used to stare at those portraits of admirals and commanding officers and wonder if that were the only way people would remember you. Back then, I thought legacy was measured in plaques and titles. But over time, I realized legacy is built every single day, in the choices you make, the people you influence, and the cycles you break. Legacy isn't just about what you leave behind.

I can still remember walking down the p-ways of my early commands, staring at the portraits of decorated leaders framed on the walls. Their smiles looked permanent, their uniforms crisp, their plaques polished, as if their stories were written in stone. I would imagine my picture there one day, chasing that image as if it were the finish line. Back then, I thought that was what legacy meant, being immortalized in a frame. But the longer I served, the more I realized how many names weren't on the wall, how much quiet greatness went unrecorded. Legacy, I learned, isn't about whether your photo makes it into a hallway; it's about how you leave people feeling when you walk out of a room.

It's about what you build while you are still here.

And I'm building mine every single day through my work, my daughter, my voice, and every Sailor I pour into.

I used to think legacy had to be this big, dramatic thing: your name on a building, a historic achievement, a headline. But now I know better.

Legacy can be quiet.

Legacy is the junior Sailor who finally believes in herself because of something I said.

It's in the mom who sees my story and realizes she can start over.

It's in my daughter growing up knowing she can take up space without apologizing.

Legacy is how you live.

How do you show up when no one is clapping?

How you stand when your name isn't in lights.

Some Sailors have come to me years later and said, "I watched how you moved. I modeled my career after you."

And I had no idea.

Because I was trying to survive-trying to make it through the next duty day, the following season, the next moment without breaking.

But they were watching.

They were learning.

My example shaped them—even when I didn't have it all figured out.

There's not a single person I've met that I haven't impacted in some way.

Sailors still call me all the time-for advice, guidance, and truth.

I've mentored countless sailors, not just by assignment–but by example.

I've been asked to reenlist sailors often, and one who told me directly:

"Ma'am, when I got to the command, you were the only one pushing me and trying to help me move forward. I will never forget everything you did for my family and me, and I would be honored to have you as my reenlisting officer. They don't make 'em like you.

When he asked me, my first instinct was shock; I had never pictured myself being chosen for something so personal and meaningful. The night of the reenlistment, the steakhouse buzzed with laughter and the smell of grilled meat, the clinking of glasses echoing around us. As I stood there, facing him with his family watching proudly. I felt a lump rise in my throat. I raised my hand, steady but emotional, and recited the oath with him, line by line. When we finished, the room erupted into applause, but what stayed with me was the look in his eyes: gratitude, trust, and belief. That moment confirmed that leadership isn't about rank alone. It's about being the person someone can trust to stand beside them as they recommit their life to service.

I'll never forget that steakhouse, the sizzle of food in the background, the clinking of glasses, the dim lights that gave the moment a quiet intimacy. I stood there in uniform, holding my hand steady as I raised it beside my Sailor, who had chosen me to usher them into another chapter of their career. When we finished, their family thanked me, eyes wet with pride, saying they knew their loved one was in good hands. Humbled me to my core. No flags were waving, no salutes lined up, no medals being pinned. Just trust, respect, and the kind of leadership that can't be ordered, only earned.

We were at a steakhouse for the ceremony, and he was so full of emotion over how far he had come. The smell of grilled steak lingered in the air, laughter rose between toasts, but in that moment, all I heard was the pride in his voice. His hands shook slightly as he raised them, steadying only as the oath left his lips.

Laughter and pride filled the room, and every smile reflected how far he'd come. And I stood there beaming – proud of the man he had become. I watched him raise his right hand, his voice filled with so much pride and strength. When we exchanged those reenlistment words, it felt like we were sealing everything we had both overcome – his growth, my leadership, and everything in between.

And when I hear that, it humbles me every single time.

Because I remember being the one looking for someone to believe in.

And now, I am that someone.

That's the thing about legacy.

It doesn't wait until you're perfect.

It starts the moment you decide to be intentional.

Now, when I show up, I show up differently. Not to impress. Not to prove anything. But to plant something in the room.

I remember a sailor who came to me from the deck division because he struck a Yeoman. I worked with him day in and day out, taught him everything I knew. When he earned his air pin, he asked me to pin him. He said he was grateful for everything I was teaching him and went on to excel at his following commands. I received phone calls and messages from others saying, "Thank you for the beast you created." I laughed when I read it, but deep down, I understood what he meant. I'd pushed him to see what he was capable of.

He was timid, awkward, and tucked into a shell when I first met him. He avoided eye contact at first, always looking at the floor when he spoke, his hands shoved deep in his pockets like he wanted to disappear. His voice was barely above a whisper, and every instruction seemed to weigh him down. I started small, asking him to brief me on routine paperwork, encouraging him to speak just a little louder each time. Slowly, I saw flickers of change. But as we worked together, and as I challenged him, I saw him shift. I think, in his heart, he just wanted to make me proud. And he did. I remember how hard he worked to master correspondence and awards – he was terrified of public speaking, but I made him brief leadership weekly. By the end, he was standing tall in meetings and commanding respect as if he were born to do it. That breakthrough told me everything: confidence grows when someone believes in you, even before you believe in yourself.

Watching him step into his own power reminded me why I never gave up, proof that seeds we plant grow even when we can't see them right away.

Watching him grow was like watching a mirror of my younger self, quiet, overlooked, unsure if his voice even mattered. I saw myself in the way he hesitated before speaking, in the way he deferred to others even when he had the right answer. That's why his transformation mattered so much to me. It wasn't just about his confidence; it was about redemption, about proving to both of us that leadership can be taught, courage can be cultivated, and confidence can be built brick by brick. Every time he raised his chin a little higher, I felt my own purpose affirmed.

Wisdom. Strength. Permission.

Because I remember being the woman who needed all of that.

I still carry scars–but I have light now, too.

There was a time I almost walked away from it all. The weight of proving myself, the whispers, the politics, it piled up so high that I wondered if it was worth it. I remember sitting in my car outside the command, hands gripping the steering wheel, tears blurring my vision. For a moment, I thought about never walking back in, but I did. And every time I see the scars left from those days, I remind myself that they are proof of survival. What once almost broke me now fuels me. Those scars shine like warning lights and guideposts, helping me lead others through storms I've already weathered.

There were days the weight almost crushed me. Nights, I sat in my car outside the command, gripping the steering wheel, whispering prayers to get through the door. There were times I plastered on a smile, walked into the building, and performed like everything was fine, only to break down in silence later. Those scars are invisible to most, but I carry them like tattoos etched into my spirit. And because I know that pain, I can see it in others before they even say a word. That empathy, born out of my own bruises, has become one of my greatest tools as a leader.

And I make sure to pass it on.

That's my legacy. Not just what I've overcome, but what I've inspired others to believe they can overcome, too

And that legacy lives on in my daughter.

She's me–but louder, bolder, and more beautifully self-assured.

She works hard, she's a cheerleader, and a beast in the pool.

I'll never forget one particular swim meet where she launched off the block with a power that made the crowd gasp. Stroke after stroke, she cut through the water with fierce determination, her arms slicing forward like she was chasing more than just the finish line. When she touched the wall and lifted her head, I saw fire in her eyes, the same fire I've carried my whole career. Another time, at a cheer competition, she nailed a tumbling pass that had the whole gym erupting. Watching her flip and land with a grin, I thought to myself, this is a legacy in motion. She is the embodiment of resilience, discipline, and joy, all the things I prayed she would inherit, without the pain I had to endure to learn them.

In that moment, I saw pieces of myself in her, her grit, her determination, the way she refused to quit until she nailed it. But I also saw something I didn't have at her age: freedom. She wasn't carrying the same weight I had carried, the same fear of being overlooked or silenced. She was just a little girl chasing her joy, unapologetic in her pursuit of excellence. And that was the greatest relief of all, to know that I was breaking the cycle, that she would inherit my fire but not chains.

One day, I went to her school, and the front office lady looked at me and said:

Ma'am, your daughter is such a beautiful person. And let me tell you something – you will never have to worry about her. That girl is going to be something. You are raising a superstar.

And in that moment, I knew:

She is my living legacy. She is the proof that healing matters, that breaking cycles isn't just about me but about giving her the freedom I never had.

That's how I know the cycle is breaking, that healing is working. Because of everything I've survived, she won't have to. That is legacy in motion, not waiting for monuments or medals, but watching cycles break and new futures rise in real time. Legacy isn't a monument waiting at the end of our careers – it's the living, breathing impact we make along the way. Every Sailor who stands taller, every daughter who walks freer, every truth we choose to live – those are the echoes that outlive us. I didn't realize it then, but legacy wasn't just about what I left for her; it was also what I reclaimed for myself.

CHAPTER 25

BECOMING THE WOMAN I NEEDED

For years, I thought the story of my life would shift the moment someone else came along and "rescued" me. I pictured a partner who would finally take the weight off my shoulders, who would notice when I was tired, who would step in when I was drowning. I remember sitting on the edge of my bed in my twenties, staring at my phone, waiting for a call that never came, waiting for someone to see me, to choose me, to show up. Every time it didn't happen, I told myself to hold on a little longer. That waiting kept me small, kept me silent, and almost made me believe I couldn't save myself.

Those years of waiting left their fingerprints on every relationship I entered. I accepted crumbs and called it love because I didn't believe I deserved more. I silenced myself in arguments to keep the peace, convincing myself that quiet suffering was better than being left alone. I told myself that if I loved harder, gave more, bent further, maybe then I would finally be chosen. But all that did was teach me to abandon myself in hopes someone else wouldn't. That kind of waiting is its own prison, and I had lived in it for far too long.

There was a time I just wanted someone to save me-to notice me, to protect me, to see the pain behind my silence and the strength in my survival.

But no one came.

So, I became her myself.

The woman I needed.

The one who speaks truth without shrinking.

The one who sets boundaries and keeps them.

The one who loves her daughter fiercely yet knows that loving herself is just as important.

I became the woman who says "no" without guilt.

Who walks away when something costs her peace.

Who gives grace – but never gives herself away for free.

As much as I have been through, sometimes I sit in silence and think of everything meant to break me and how I freed myself from every single one.

I remember being the "go-to" for people I couldn't go to.

I remember letting people borrow things and never getting them back in how I gave them.

I remember my car being wrecked by a family member, and I had to eat that.

I remember being run over emotionally, drained, and depleted.

And then one day, someone asked me for help, and I was too tired. I looked them in the eye and said, "No."

The word felt heavy in my mouth, like it carried years of swallowed pain with it. For a second, the room went still. Their eyebrows lifted in surprise, maybe even disbelief, as if they couldn't fathom me refusing. My heart pounded so loudly I could hear it in my ears, but I didn't flinch. My shoulders squared, my breath steadied, and in that silence, I realized I had just redrawn the map of my life with one word. "No" was more than a refusal; it was a declaration that I belonged to myself.

That "No" wasn't just about him; it echoed back to the little girl who had been taught not to rock the boat, to bite her tongue, to keep everyone comfortable even when it hurt her. Saying "No" was like reaching back through time and pulling her out of silence, telling her she deserved better. For the first time, I wasn't afraid of disappointing someone else. I was more afraid of betraying myself. That moment was small to anyone watching, but to me, it was revolutionary. It was the day my voice stopped being negotiable.

No overexplaining. No guilt. Just – no.

Each day and each time someone expected more from me, I continued to say no. It hurt – almost pained me – because I was always the "yes," even when I wanted to say no, even to my daughter. But I knew I had to stop being the yes woman. It wasn't helping them or me, and I realized it was draining me mentally, physically, and emotionally. I was just tired – and I had to choose differently.

It felt so good, it became my new word.

I stopped waiting to be chosen.

I stopped hoping they'd change.

I stopped breaking my own heart to keep the peace.

And peace, for me, is no noise. I enjoy silence now. I enjoy not doing anything. There used to be days when I always had to stay busy – work, home, errands, always in motion. I was dragging myself everywhere when what I truly needed was rest. I even took the TV out of my room because it was too noisy; I didn't want to hear it anymore. At first, the silence was jarring. No hum of voices in the background, no endless noise to drown out my thoughts. Just quiet. But in that quiet, I found something I never knew I craved, safety. I would light a candle, sit on my bed, and listen to the stillness, where once silence had felt lonely, now it wrapped around me like protection. The absence of chaos became my sanctuary, a reminder that peace doesn't always come with sound; it often lives in the quiet we once ran from. The silence felt great. It was perfect. It wasn't emptiness, it was evidence of healing. I had finally learned to exist in my own company.

The quiet became sacred. I would light a candle in the evenings, the faint smell of "vanilla filling the room" as I curled up on the couch with a blanket. I could hear the hum of the refrigerator, the rhythm of my own breathing, even the steady beat of my heart, things I had never noticed before because chaos had always drowned them out. That silence wasn't empty; it was proof that I was safe, that my peace no longer depended on anyone else's presence or absence. It was mine, and for the first time, I trusted myself to protect it.

I would sit on the edge of my bed in that quiet, no-TV, no-noise, and realize this was what safety sounded like. Not chaos. Not fear. Just me, breathing.

Instead, I chose myself.

And it changed everything.

I no longer survive storms; I outgrow them.

I no longer measure myself by what I do for others; I lead from overflow.

I wake up in a home that feels like mine.

I parent with presence, not pain.

I work from purpose, not pressure.

And most of all, I give that younger version of me everything she never had:

Peace.

Safety.

Joy.

Pride.

And a voice that no one can mute.

One day, I caught my daughter watching me in the mirror as I got ready. She didn't say a word, just studied me closely, as if she were memorizing the way I carried myself. In that moment, I realized she wasn't just seeing her mother, she was witnessing the healed, unapologetic woman I had fought to become. She was learning, silently, that it's possible to rebuild, to choose yourself, to rise. Becoming "her" wasn't just for the little girl inside me; it was also for the little girl standing right in front of me.

I'll never forget the way she looked at me in that moment, her eyes wide, her smile soft, like she was memorizing me. She mirrored my stance without even realizing it, straightening her back, lifting her chin. And in that instant, I knew the work I had done wasn't just for me. She was absorbing every lesson I hadn't spoken, every truth I had lived. She was watching what it looked like for a woman to rise, to heal, to stand unapologetically in her own worth. And I felt a wave of relief knowing she wouldn't have to search as long as I did for that example.

The black sheep they once overlooked now stands crowned in her own becoming.

I became her.

I am her.

I'm still becoming – louder, softer, wiser, freer – every day.

And as much as I became her for myself and for my daughter, I also became her for every woman who has ever felt unseen, unheard, or unworthy. This book is my offering, my proof that survival can turn into thriving, that silence can transform into song, and that brokenness can give birth to wholeness. I don't have all the answers, but I have my truth, and that's what I'll keep giving, over and over. Because becoming her isn't a destination. It's a choice I make, boldly and deliberately, every single day.

And if you're reading this, waiting for someone to rescue you, I want you to know what I finally learned: no one is coming. But that isn't bad news, it's the best news. Because the woman you've been waiting for is already inside you. She's waiting for you to trust her, to choose her, to let her lead. Becoming her doesn't happen overnight; it happens in the small decisions, the quiet boundaries, the brave "No's" that redraw your map. Don't wait as long as I did.

Choose yourself now. Become her now, and when you do, the world around you will have no choice but to rise to meet her because you are enough, exactly as you are.

About the Author

Diana M. Martin is a United States Navy Officer whose journey from enlisted to commissioned officer reflects both resilience and transformation. With more than seventeen years of dedicated service, she has built her career through discipline, grit, and an unwavering commitment to growth.

Beyond the uniform, Diana is a mother, mentor, and advocate for healing and generational change. She believes deeply in the power of rewriting your narrative, speaking your truth, and using your story to light the way for others to navigate their own storms.

Her writing blends vulnerability with strength, offering readers a space to feel seen, understood, and empowered. Diana's mission is to remind others that no matter where you begin, you have the ability to rise, not flawless, not untouched, but unbreakable.

Unbreakable is her most personal and powerful work to date.

SCAN THE QR CODE TO STAY IN TOUCH AND LEARN MORE ABOUT MY JOURNEY